921/COU

David
Coulthard

David
Coulthard

His decade in Formula 1

Anthony Rowlinson

Foreword by Sir Frank Williams

Dedication
For my family

First published in January 2004

A catalogue record for this book is available from the
British Library.

Published by Haynes Publishing,
Sparkford, Yeovil, Somerset BA22 7JJ

Tel: 01963 442030 Fax: 01963 440001
Int. tel: +44 1963 442030 Int.fax: +44 1963 440001
E-mail: sales@haynes.co.uk
Website: www.haynes.co.uk

ISBN 1 84425 035 0

Library of Congress catalog card number 2003113465

*All photographs are from the LAT archive unless
otherwise stated.*

Haynes North America Inc.
861 Lawrence Drive, Newbury Park,
California 91320, USA

Page layout by James Robertson
Printed and bound by J. H. Haynes & Co. Ltd., Sparkford

contents

foreword 7

introduction and acknowledgements 8

1 ticket to ride 10

2 the long and winding road 22

3 drive my car 32

4 with a little help from my friends 56

5 fixing a hole 68

6 money – that's what I want 80

7 when i'm 64 94

8 help! 108

9 yesterday 122

10 tomorrow never knows 138

results 148

index 152

prelude

Tantalus

Tantalus was punished… with eternal torment. Now he hangs, perenially consumed by thirst and hunger, from the bough of a fruit tree, which leans over a marshy lake. Its waves lap against his waist, and sometimes reach his chin, yet whenever he bends down to drink, they slip away, and nothing remains but the black mud at his feet; or, if he ever succeeds in scooping up a handful of water, it slips through his fingers before he can do more than wet his cracked lips, leaving him thirstier than ever. The tree is laden with pears, shining apples, sweet figs, ripe olives, and pomegranates, which dangle against his shoulders; but whenever he reaches for the luscious fruit, a gust of wind whirls them out of his reach.[1]

Sisyphus

Sisyphus was shown a huge block of stone and ordered to roll it up to the brow of a hill and topple it down the farther slope. He has never yet succeeded in doing so. As soon as he has almost reached the summit, he is forced back by the weight of the shameless stone, which bounces to the very bottom once more; where he wearily retrieves it and must begin all over again, though sweat bathes his limbs, and a cloud of dust rises above his head.[2]

[1] Robert Graves, *The Greek Myths* (Penguin, 1992).
[2] Ibid.

It's never easy being a Formula 1 driver but for ten years David Coulthard has managed to avoid the worst of the pitfalls.

foreword

by Sir Frank Williams

David came to my attention after a really strong season in Formula 3, and he certainly didn't disappoint when he took up testing duties for Williams in 1993. He was studious, serious and determined, all of which conspired to make him an immensely capable character in the cockpit.

The events of 1994 threw Williams, quite naturally, into complete turmoil. It is my absolute conviction that very few other young protagonists could have effectively stepped up to the plate in such terrible circumstances, but David displayed a maturity in his debut season that I regard as one of his hallmarks.

In his first race for Williams in Spain, sadly curtailed by an ignition failure, he demonstrated a skill that I have always admired – his brilliant starts – and he characteristically claimed three places off the Catalunya grid. His reaction time is unparalleled in the sport, and that is some accolade considering the company he keeps on a Formula 1 grid every fortnight. There is no more impressive a sight than the unleashing of thousands of horsepower in a cacophony of noise and smoke, especially if there is a Scottish scythe in the midst of it all, carving his way to turn one like a man possessed.

In his second appearance for the team in Canada, the FW16 behaved and he was immediately among the points. His performance in Montreal, I sensed at that time, was immediately indicative of a long and noteworthy career ahead in Formula 1.

I figure I had a kinship with David perhaps due to my ten formative years spent at school in Castle Douglas, not a million miles away from Twynholm, but my inclination towards him as a sportsman runs deeper than those characteristically Scottish virtues of discipline and dedication. As he has demonstrated on many occasions during his career, it would appear as if David had emerged from a bygone era when sportsmanship was the mark of a man.

Some may characterise David's absence of sporting vice as a weakness, but I would regard such a view as incomplete. DC's best performances – for example his win in Italy in 1997 – rank him among Formula 1's elite guard, and a rare example of what history will remember as sublime talent with manners.

In their hour of greatest need Williams, the most hard-headed of teams, had made what seemed a romantic decision: to give the youngster a chance in recognition of all his hard work in testing. [Sutton Motorsport]

introduction
and acknowledgements

In a Formula 1 career spanning a decade, David Coulthard has established himself as one of the sport's very best competitors. Although, at the time of writing, still uncrowned as a World Champion, he has proved himself absolutely worthy of a place in the F1 elite, and his record bears comparison with that of many of the acknowledged 'greats'.

Throughout a rich, turbulent career, DC, as he is fondly known, has never been less than an articulate, engaging individual, whose conduct on and off the track has earned him a legion of admirers. Yet his goal remains elusive. The concluding chapters of his extraordinary story are still to be written.

I should like to thank each of the following for their time, guidance and kindness in helping me write this book:

Miriam Baker, Cynthia Belcher, Matt Bishop, Ann Bradshaw, David Boyce, Thomas 'Jeremy' Clarkson, Jock Clear, Liam Clogger, Laura Coppin, Didier Coton, Lynsay Coulthard, Sarah Edworthy, Gil de Ferran, Peter Foubister, Kika Garcia-Concheso, Anna Guerrier, Will Griffiths, Mark Gallagher, Celia Garrett, George Gribbin, Silvia Hoffer, John Hogan, Mika Hakkinen, Peter Higham, Mark Hughes, Eddie Judd, Emily Kearns, David Leslie, Mike Levitt, Bill MacDonald, Allan McNish, Robin Miller, Sheila Mutch, Flora Myer, Mel Nichols, Rebecca Nichols, Jon Noble, Tracy Novak, Paige Pell, Jo Ramirez, Lara Richards, Donna Robertson, staff at the Pitstop Diner in Twynholm, Stéphane Samson, John Smithies, Paul Stewart, Sir Jackie Stewart, Dave Stubbs, David Taylor, Steven Tee, Richard West, Keith Wiggins, Sir Frank Williams, Stewart Williams, Kevin Wood, Jim Wright, Simon Wright, Tim Wright, Tim Wright (LAT).

Several others, who prefer to remain anonymous, have given invaluable assistance. My thanks to you all.

Special thanks, above all, go to Michelle, for putting up with late nights, lost weekends and grumpiness. Love as always.

Anthony Rowlinson, 2004

In an era notable for the domination of Michael Schumacher and the Ferrari team, David put up some serious challenges.

David brought youth, enthusiasm, and determination to Williams in his role as test driver in 1993. He quickly found himself accepted as part of the team, but at this stage he could have no idea of the dramatic incidents which would lead to his F1 race debut.

ticket to ride

The British Airways Boeing 757 from Heathrow to Barcelona touched down just after 3pm on Wednesday, 25 May 1994. The private jet with its familiar faces in the cockpit would come later; for now, this was the best plane in the world. It was the plane transporting David Coulthard to his first grand prix as a Formula 1 racing driver. The keys to a Renault Laguna were waiting for him at the Europcar desk. In less than an hour he would arrive at the Circuit de Catalunya as a competitor. By Sunday he would know, at last, what it meant to sit on a Formula 1 grid amid 25 equally determined, almost equally talented, rivals, and take the start (and, with luck, the finish) of a grand prix. Everything that had gone before was just preparation.

He knew he could drive. He had proved, too, that he could handle a Formula 1 car with a deft, subtle touch: 1993 and the early months of '94 had been spent dovetailing a race programme in the sub-F1 Formula 3000 championship with a full schedule of test driving for the Williams F1 team. David had carried out 25 major tests for them in '93; he helped develop that year's Williams-Renault FW15C well enough to allow lead driver Alain Prost to sashay to his fourth world title. With Damon Hill as Prost's number two, Williams became dominant winners of the year's constructors' title as well – their 168 points neatly doubling the 84 of second-placed McLaren.

David had hurled himself at the test drive opportunity when it arose. It was a hint of a way in to the exclusive Formula 1 world. It also provided a welcome leg up for a career which had threatened to stall after two disappointing Formula 3000 seasons. Even so, his lot was far from ideal. Test drivers grind out thousands of thankless kilometres around race tracks in a non-competitive situation, often for reasons which a team doesn't make clear ('Can't let the driver know what we're doing. He might, you know, tell someone'). Their blessing, however, is to allow a Formula 1 *ingénue*, as David was, the time and space to practise their skills. Mistakes can be made backstage; speed learned before it is demanded. The aim was to be fast and fluent – and never to bend the car.

Every now and again there might be a chance to show a bit of pace: test team manager Brian Lambert might, if the schedule allowed, permit a run in the early evening shade, on low fuel and a set of sticky tyres. David might, then, finish the day with the confidence boost of a good lap time; he might see that, yes, he really could live with the established stars. Who knows? One day the team might be impressed enough to give their youngster a drive in the race car. That's what had happened with Damon Hill, after all, Williams's understudy in '92, their race driver in '93.

It didn't look as if anything similar would happen for David this time around. Not with Ayrton Senna having joined Williams for '94 alongside Damon Hill. The team had their ace and their super-competent, fast-improving number two. David would have to look elsewhere for a Formula 1 race drive this year.

He had finished third in the Formula 3000 championship in '93, behind Olivier Panis and Pedro Lamy, both of whom went on to drive in F1. He knew that only a step up to F1, either as a full-time test driver with a major team, or in a race seat with a lesser rival, would maintain his career momentum. He knew too that Williams liked him, rated him, even. Repeat invitations to test their precious racing cars were a rubber stamp of his ability. He was becoming part of the family. At one test, at the French Paul Ricard circuit, Williams's mechanics decided to display their affection in their own unique manner.

David had spent the day tearing around the track in a variety of Renault road cars with corporate guests at his side. The thrill-seeking passengers got a memorable day out, while the good relations between Williams and their engine supplier were promoted, subliminally. Chauffeur duties over, David headed back to his rental car to return to the airport, and home. As he got nearer the car, he was surprised, but flattered, to see how many Williams staff had come to wave him off.

Suspecting nothing, he got into the car and turned the ignition key. Two high-pressure jets of water gushed out from beneath the dashboard, drenching his khaki chino trousers in the most embarrassing fashion. This was mechanics' sabotage at its finest. Earlier in the day they had re-arranged the car's screenwash plumbing to direct it through the dashboard and straight at the driver. They had also tweaked the electrics, to activate the washers at the first turn of the key.

David stepped from the car, sodden, speechless.

Ann Bradshaw, Williams's press officer, remembers the look on David's face: 'You hear of people's jaw dropping in surprise. Well, David's really had. His mouth was hanging open in disbelief. He just didn't know what to say. I think eventually he stammered something about not having another pair of trousers, which of course had us all howling with laughter. We had already been reduced to tears at the sight of this huge wet patch around his crotch.'

There had been other, more serious, signs of good faith. When the team unveiled their '94 colours, designed around new multi-million dollar title sponsors, Rothmans, David was the driver chosen to give the freshly-painted FW15 its first run in public. For a 22-year-old clinging to the racing ladder, saddled with debt and with few resources other than a well of self-belief, it was a huge vote of confidence.

He had also recently negotiated a retained testing deal for '94 (his previous work had all been on a freelance basis), so in small but significant ways Williams were acknowledging that David was part of the team. He certainly looked the part that day at Estoril in Portugal, his blue and white saltire helmet – designed and painted by old karting buddy Brian Smith – perfectly complementing the team's new image.

But still, whichever way David looked at Williams's race team arrangements for '94, three into two wouldn't go.

On 27 March the F1 season got under way in Brazil, the Williams cars being driven by Senna and Hill. By

By 1994 Ayrton Senna had become the iconic Formula 1 driver, and his arrival at Williams that year promised to enhance his reputation still further. He possessed a unique ability to articulate the sensation of driving a Formula 1 car at and beyond its limit. Sometimes, he said, it was akin to an out-of-body experience. Here, he's ahead of Michael Schumacher early in the fateful 1994 race at Imola.

mid-April, with the start of the F3000 season barely a fortnight away, David took stock of his limited options and signed to drive for the hard-up Vortex team, resigning himself to another year with the wannabes. He drove for them only once.

Ayrton Senna was killed on 1 May 1994. He died after a 190mph (305kph) accident at the Tamburello corner of the Imola circuit, in the tiny Italian principality of San Marino, 45 miles (72km) from Bologna.

Senna was that rarest of sporting icons: a truly global star. He was arguably the world's most famous sportsman; a competitor as feared by his rivals as he was respected; an individual of deep spirituality. He was Williams's lead driver. He was going to be the '94 World Champion.

By coincidence his signature, with two dozen others, was on a fax sent by the Williams team to David on the morning of 1 May, wishing him good luck in that day's F3000 race at Silverstone. The fax is still on display in a glass cabinet at the David Coulthard museum in David's home town of Twynholm. It reads (all in capital letters):

ATTENTION DAVID COULTHARD
ALL BEST WISHES FROM
EVERYONE AT THE
ROTHMANS WILLIAMS RENAULT TEAM

Among the messages are those of Ayrton Senna ('Very best to you'); Damon Hill's wife, Georgie; 'The Fat Bastard Paul'; and Uncle Iain (with 'hugs and kisses').

The death of Ayrton Senna cast shadows over F1 that eclipsed the sport for a time. Nowhere was the darkness more absolute than at Williams, where hopes of a wonderful racing partnership had been so high. Senna had described joining Williams as 'a dream come true'. Frank Williams, he said, 'was the man who gave me my first opportunity to drive an F1 car. It is ten years since that test, and now, finally, we've come together.' Frank had been similarly delighted: 'I have always wanted Ayrton to drive for Williams because he is an outstanding champion. I have been talking to him for ten years and suddenly there was an opportunity.'

After Senna's death it fell to Frank and the team's co-founder, Patrick Head, to re-light the torch. Once lit, it was passed to Damon Hill to carry. With remarkable courage he finished sixth at Imola, in the race restarted after Senna's accident. A fortnight later, he raced as the team's sole entry at Monaco. The burden was mighty for a man whose F1 race experience amounted to little more than two seasons, and whose own ex-double World Champion father, Graham, had also been killed prematurely.

Another torch was handed to David in the Paddock Club of Barcelona's Circuit de Catalunya, where, at 3.30pm on the Thursday before the '94 Spanish Grand

The 1994 San Marino Grand Prix threw Formula 1 into turmoil. The death of Roland Ratzenberger in practice was followed by the death of Senna in the race a day later. The cause of each accident is still to be fully explained.

Prix, Frank Williams announced that Coulthard would, that weekend, step up to the race team. 'I chose David,' grinned Sir Frank, thinly, 'because he has an absolutely gorgeous girlfriend' (model Andrea Murray).

In their hour of greatest need, this most pragmatic, hard-headed, even ruthless, of teams had made what seemed a romantic decision: it appeared the youngster had been given a chance in recognition of all his hard work in testing. There was an element of that, of course, and David had certainly shown pace and intelligence at the wheel.

His gratitude was genuine, unforced, though not starry-eyed: 'Testing for Williams was a huge opportunity. Racing for them is an even bigger one.' 'Thanks for the chance, guys,' seemed to be the message, 'I know I can do the job.' But changing a Senna-Hill combination to a Hill-Coulthard pairing could only weaken a team with explicit world title aspirations. For all David's talent and ambition, he was not the lamented triple World Champion, the man reckoned by some to have been the greatest driver ever. The gamble Williams were taking by thrusting a fresh-faced novice into the most high-profile race seat in Formula 1 was not lost on them.

Secretly, Sir Frank had entered negotiations with

Nigel Mansell, Williams's '92 World Champion, to return as a standard bearer and help support Damon Hill's quest for the '94 drivers' title. Notoriously high maintenance, Mansell had left Williams in a fit of pique at the end of '92, when the team declined to accede to some of his more extreme contractual requests, such as their meeting the bill for luxury hotel suites at every race. He fled to America, lured by $12 million from American industrialist and Indycar team owner Carl Haas, and set about fuelling his legend by winning the '93 Indycar title. He was still there, preparing for the '94 Indianapolis 500 race, when Frank Williams picked up the phone and offered him a $9 million, eight-race deal to come back and race for Williams until the end of the season. At the time, Mansell was contracted with the Newman-Haas team to race alongside Mario Andretti until the end of '95, but Carl Haas hinted he would consider releasing Mansell for the six remaining grands prix that did not clash with Indycar rounds.

F1, as always, needed 'box office' and Nigel 'limelight' Mansell was nothing if not good box office. 'I never wanted Nigel to leave in the first place,' said F1 impresario Bernie Ecclestone at the time. 'He's young enough to make a comeback, it would be good for him. It would also be better for F1 if we get someone to take on Schumacher. Now it's up to Nigel, but if I can make it happen I will.'[1]

Mansell's former Williams team-mate, Italian veteran Riccardo Patrese, had also been mentioned as a safe pair of hands until the end of the year, but he ruled himself out of the drive, saying he had been too saddened by Senna's death to want any further part in Formula 1. Only Mansell, then, had appeared to be an obstacle to David's F1 debut.

In the event, Mansell did not drive at Barcelona, Williams's offer having come too late for contract negotiations to be resolved in time for the Spanish Grand Prix. In fact, he only drove four races for the team in '94. The 'will he, won't he' saga would provide a theatrical diversion for the rest of the season, but for the Barcelona weekend at least, the Williams drive was David's – as was a majestic fee of £5,000. F1 team principals are nothing if not tough with a buck. Coulthard's deal was on a 'race by race' basis and covered the Spanish Grand Prix only. The unspoken incentive for him was that, should he conduct himself with sufficient aplomb, further 'one-offs' would be considered.

David showed his usual outward calm in the week before his Formula 1 debut: this tester-about-to-become-racer was fully aware of the fates swirling around him, but all he could do was strap himself in, step on the gas, and set the times. But there *was* pressure – although DC didn't acknowledge it in the days before his race drive was made definite: 'I'm not under any pressure just now, until anything is confirmed to me. As and when it is confirmed, then I guess there will be an increase in pressure. I'm very aware that the overall impression you give at your first grand prix means you're either there or you're not. That's on my mind, but as long as I do the best I can and I'm honest with myself and the team, then I'll be comfortable with that.'[2]

Frank Williams (left) turned to his test driver following the death of Senna.

From the very beginning, Coulthard, here with Williams technical director Patrick Head, was confident in expressing his opinions. The team quickly learned to value his detailed technical analysis of his car's behaviour.

After Senna's death, Williams and engine partners Renault were keen to lure back the proven championship-winning talents of Nigel Mansell. Mansell had been crowned World Champion in 1992 with Williams-Renault, but quit F1 at the end of that year to race in America.

David was fast in his first race and proved well capable of racing wheel-to-wheel with fellow future stars Michael Schumacher and Mika Häkkinen. He did enough in that first race to convince the team to give him another run.

Williams tested for three days at the Jerez circuit in southern Spain in the run up to the Barcelona race. On the Sunday afternoon, precisely one week before he would make his first F1 start, Coulthard gave his Williams a hefty whack, wiping off the right-front corner and necessitating an hour with a physio later in the day. He wouldn't admit it – racing drivers never do – but he had been trying hard because he knew that the day of reckoning was fast approaching, the moment when he would be measured against the only two arbiters that matter: stopwatch and team-mate. The atmosphere in the team had changed that week, as they started to look for a way out of the abyss in which they had found themselves post-Imola.

Suddenly David was being encouraged to set faster times in testing, to show his hand, to push – both himself and de facto team leader Hill. A few broken parts matter not to a team if their driver is quick. 'Everyone wanted me to push harder,' he said, 'they wanted to know what my full potential was.'

So did David. After driving all his testing miles in the '93 car, FW15, he was itching to get a proper run in the latest Williams, the FW16 – the car he would race; the car in which Senna had been killed. It had developed a reputation as being a tricky machine to drive, twitchy, unstable, lacking grip. The sort of car which even Senna found a challenge; the sort of car a rookie would wish for a lot of time in before he had to race it. David's allocation was a handful of laps, as the last day of the Jerez test, when he had been due to go out and smoke FW16's tyres, was rained off. At least David had the comfort of working for a hard-wrought winning organisation, one where sentiment was shoved to one side as the serious business of beating the opposition was got on with.

While the team's resolve helped his mental preparations, a swirl of political turmoil in the paddock did not. Only a month had passed since the San Marino Grand Prix, and in the wake of the two deaths that weekend (Austrian Roland Ratzenberger was killed during Saturday practice) Formula 1's governing body, the FIA, had sought to impose wide-ranging technical changes with the intent of slowing the cars down and preventing further fatalities.

Formula 1 hates change. It costs money. When teams are told to 'cut downforce', for example, and thereby reduce their cars' grip – slowing them down – their engineers have to scuttle back to their computer

From his earliest days at Williams, David proved a big hit with the celebrities, like Sylvester 'Rocky' Stallone, who frequented the grands prix.

screens and wind tunnels to design new parts. Parts costing tens of thousands of pounds. The teams always object. They were objecting, strongly, throughout the Spanish Grand Prix weekend. FIA President Max Mosley, an urbane, cerebral individual, with an occasionally bloodthirsty taste for direct, intellectual confrontation, was demanding that teams make significant technical changes to their cars. He argued that the FIA had the power to do this on the grounds of safety – the only topic of paddock conversation since Imola. The teams were having none of it and on Friday morning, just as David should have been tightening his belts and flexing his palms around his FW16's tiny, suede-covered steering wheel, a quarrel of team principals squeezed their egos into the Williams motorhome to confront Mosley.

That the teams backed Mosley into a corner and forced him to agree to a revision of some of his planned rule changes mattered little to a certain Scottish Formula 1 rookie, who at that moment was waging his own war with the butterflies in his stomach. What *did* matter was that while debate continued, Frank Williams, along with several other senior team principals, including McLaren's Ron Dennis and Benetton's Flavio Briatore, had ordered his cars not to go out on track. As David sat and wondered if Formula 1 was always like this, his track

time ebbed away. In the heat and the dust of a Spanish summer, a man could be forgiven for thinking he had made a bad career turn.

Then – at last – the motorhome door cracked open and the bosses muttered their way back to their own garages. Game on. The oddly quiet paddock suddenly came alive as mechanics fired up becalmed engines in preparation for that afternoon's qualifying session.

Deprived of a useful, reassuring warm-up period, David's first laps of consequence in FW16 would be completed instead during this most difficult, challenging hour. He would have been forgiven nerves and tetchiness under the circumstances. In fact, his calm was remarkable.

Moments before he pulled out of the Williams garage to begin his qualifying laps, Patrick Head, Williams's technical director, spoke to David over the pit-to-car radio: 'OK, David, we're not looking for anything dramatic, just take the car round, keep it off the kerbs, make sure you qualify.'

'Thanks, Patrick. Remind me, when I pull out of the garage, do I turn left or right into the pit lane?'

There was no shortage of confidence or dry wit in car number 2, but David's limited time in its cockpit was a concern. Times set on Friday were significant, because should a driver not run for any reason on the Saturday, or should that day's session be rain-affected, his best Friday lap would be the one which counted. The pressure was on. David managed three hard laps, but his best time of 1m 27.428s was good enough only for 16th spot – 13 places and two-and-a-half seconds from Hill.

He admitted to having trouble feeling comfortable with the car: 'I was a bit worried about it, because I thought it might be very difficult to drive. But I seemed to get into the swing of it quite quickly, though I still don't feel able to push it, like I could the FW15.'[3]

Still, there was always tomorrow.

For a moment on Saturday morning it looked like Imola all over again. That day at San Marino, Simtek driver Roland Ratzenberger had been killed 18 minutes into practice when his car left the track at around 200mph (320kph) and hit a concrete retaining wall. It was

Andrea Montermini's huge accident at the Spanish Grand Prix followed another to Karl Wendlinger at Monaco. Formula 1 was going through a dangerous period in early 1994: Montermini was lucky to escape with light injuries, but Wendlinger lapsed into a coma and never recovered his full racing abilities.

believed to have suffered a front-wing failure. Ratzenberger, whose neck was broken in the impact, was officially recorded as having died eight minutes after arriving at Bologna's Maggiore hospital.

By the Spanish GP, his place in the team had been taken by Italian Andrea Montermini. His black and purple car, sponsored prominently by MTV, carried a strip across the top of the engine cover in the red and white stripes of Ratzenberger's helmet. It carried the words: 'For Roland'. They seemed dreadfully macabre as Montermini's own shattered car slewed to a halt in the middle of the Barcelona track, his racing boots poking through the mess of metal and carbon fibre that had been its nose and front suspension. He had hit a concrete wall at almost 140mph (225kph) after losing control at the final corner. Still shocking images show Montermini slumped forward in the cockpit of his smoking chassis, his helmet resting on his sternum. Surely he must be dead?

The paddock had remained jittery post-Imola, and only two weeks before Spain, at Monaco, another violent accident had left German driver Karl Wendlinger in a coma. Now this. Relief followed disbelief when a statement from the Hospital General de Catalunya announced that Montermini had suffered nothing worse than a broken toe and a cracked heel.

Few bothered to look at the session times after that. Those who did saw Coulthard, D., in third place,

behind Michael Schumacher and Mika Häkkinen – respectively his future nemesis and team-mate.

All racing drivers are single-minded, focused – some might even say selfish – individuals. Very few among them have the ability to shut out completely what surrounds them and concentrate on the lap, the race. Perhaps it is no coincidence that this trio would go on to be among Formula 1's leading players over the following decade. That characteristic focus which they shared was recognised in David from a very young age by fellow Scot Allan McNish, whose racing career frequently ran in parallel to Coulthard's from their first tussles together, in karts, in the early '80s.

'One of the things that was clear,' he says, 'is that he was competitive, motivated and very straightforward, and he knew what he wanted from a young age. He also came from a good background, because his father had a very similar attitude in his business career. In business or in sport, if you have that naturally it will change and shape you. If he'd had no talent in karting he would have been similarly competitive in any other field. He's quite strong-minded – he has more than proved that through his years at McLaren. You only have to look at the team-mates he's had, and the boss that he's had there [Ron Dennis]. He's well able to battle with difficult circumstances around him and come out pretty much on top.'

He didn't come out quite on top that afternoon, in final qualifying, but he did manage to squeak into the top ten, in ninth place, despite a best lap spoiled by chassis imbalance, a small mistake, and tyre pressures being too low for maximum grip. Typically, he was honest, and harder on himself than anyone else would be, acknowledging his inexperience but also expressing frustration at not being able to do better.

David's need for a perfectly balanced car in order to be able to get the best time from it would become a recurring theme throughout his F1 career – as would his compensating ability to tune a car for the race.

In race morning warm-up he was fourth fastest. A points finish in his first grand prix had become a very real possibility.

It became even more real when car number 2 leapt from ninth to sixth at the start. Schumacher's Benetton was stealing away at the front, with Hill, in second, just about in touch. Häkkinen's McLaren was right behind, then came Jean Alesi's Ferrari, JJ Lehto's Benetton and the 'astonishingly composed' Coulthard, all jostling for position between fourth and sixth. This was great stuff. In the Paddock Club hospitality area, Joyce and Duncan Coulthard, David's mum and dad, tingled with excitement as they watched their boy do good. In his back pocket Duncan could feel that his wallet was heavier than usual. This was the first race of

David's parents, Duncan and Joyce Coulthard, together here with his then girlfriend Andrea Murray, were a close-knit support team for the new F1 star. Duncan had supported David financially all the way to F3000.

David had a Formula 1 girlfriend even before he got to F1. He and Andrea share a fleeting kiss before the hero goes off to do battle. (Empics)

David's career for which it hadn't had to be emptied, to some degree.

As Hill was proving in second place, David's car should have been quicker than all those ahead of him, up to his team-mate. Fourth place seemed well within his reach, and then, who knows, maybe a scrap for the last podium spot with Häkkinen. But what no one outside the team knew was that David's FW16 was crippled by electrical problems. Its Renault engine would not pull cleanly at low revs and they feared trouble when he came in for his first pit stop. Lap 16 confirmed the worst. DC came in from sixth: tyres on; fuel in and … nothing. The engine stalled. It was fired up again. It stalled again. This most professional of new boys was being made to look amateur by a niggling electrical glitch. By the time he got back out, he had slipped to 20th place. He fought back to 12th, but the electrics were now interfering with throttle and gearbox. He was called in again, for good.

Frank Williams was effusive over David's performance, describing his driving as 'magnificent' and proclaiming him 'a new star'. The more anodyne team press release later stated: 'David lived up to all our expectations. He drove very sensibly bearing in mind he had never driven the FW16 before and showed a great deal of maturity in dealing with what was a new situation for him. He was unlucky not to have finished, but everyone was impressed with his debut, which is why we're very happy he's joining us for Canada.'

What was this? DC in for Canada? He had done enough to convince the team to give him another try. Just like that he was working his way into the F1 establishment. The mechanical problems hadn't been his fault, after all, and the team hadn't overlooked the fact that they cost David a likely third place finish.

Häkkinen and Lehto, who had been running just ahead of Coulthard, both retired also, and Alesi's race pace faded. Eventual third-placed man Mark Blundell, in the Tyrrell, had not had the speed to match any of these drivers early on, so David's first race could easily have brought a podium. Damon Hill won the grand prix, from Schumacher, and for the first time in a month the clouds over Williams parted just a little.

David had been part of this. He shared the team's emotions and he would do so again two weeks later. 'I like the challenge,' he said, 'I like the cars and I like everything about the F1 paddock. I feel I was made to be here. I hope I can stay.'

Most of the paddock hoped he could, too. But Nigel Mansell would have something to say about that.

[1] *Autosport*, 26 May 1994.

[2] Ibid.

[3] *Autosport*, 2 June 1994.

David was almost immediately successful in karts. Here, aged 12, he's collecting a trophy for winning the Scottish Junior Karting Championship in 1983. Note the grubby fingernails! (Courtesy of the David Coulthard Museum)

the long and winding road

'You know, when dad bought him his first kart for his birthday, he wasn't really that keen on the idea. Dad said to him: "Oh, go on, have a go, you might like it." I think he was right.'

Lynsay Coulthard's childhood recollections of her big brother are close and fond. Revealing, too: who would have thought a young DC would be reluctant to get into his first kart? 'It's strange to think of,' she laughs, 'but that's how it was. I have to remind myself of it now, because once he worked out that he liked it, that was it. He was obsessed. He was 11 then, I was only five, so from then on all I can remember is David racing. You don't remember much before you're five, do you, so almost all my memories of David are of him being involved in karting or going racing.'

They grew up, with eldest brother Duncan, mum Joyce, and dad (also Duncan), in Twynholm, Kircudbrightshire, south-west Scotland. It's a place stuck in size somewhere between hamlet and village. It's a place stuck in time somewhere between the industrial revolution and the twenty-first century. Not much changes there. Not much has ever changed. There are two pubs, a post office, a church, a cemetery; The David Coulthard Museum and Pit Stop

This sweet-looking child, tie askew around his half-in, half-out collar, is David Marshall Coulthard, aged eight. Twenty years later he was a world famous millionaire. (Courtesy of the David Coulthard Museum)

diner. Fewer than 400 people live there. One of the pubs, the Star Hotel, has stood where it stands since sometime early in the 1700s. Landlord Jim Barrie will slap the granite walls proudly for visitors, pointing out their great depth. 'They could build then, aye. The roof beams are all dovetailed, too. There's no nails in there.'

One corner of the pub is dedicated to David. Glass-fronted shelving displays a helmet, a clutch of racing pictures, sundry other DC knick-knacks. 'We get 80 or more people in here on a Sunday to watch David,' says Jim. 'Some of them run up Scottish Saltires outside their homes if he's done well. He's very much the local hero. Still comes in a for an orange juice at Christmas.'

Twynholm is a gentle place. The pace of life there isn't so much slow as non-existent. Life just … is. It's an unlikely birthplace for a Formula 1 star, but then, where do racing drivers come from, if not from here, there, anywhere? Jim Clark was from Duns, in the eastern Borders, a village as agricultural as Twynholm; Jackie Stewart was a Dumbarton lad, from way over west between Glasgow and Loch Lomond. On 27 March 1971, Twynholm welcomed a son, David Marshall Coulthard, who would lend this otherwise invisible collection of homes a sense of place beyond their boundaries.

David wasn't the first Twynholm Coulthard of note. The family name is writ large there – literally, in fact, thanks to their road haulage business located in the village centre. Visitors reach Twynholm from the A75, turning into an unclassified country lane and following it downhill, to be met with a series of metre-high red letters typed into the skyline: HAYTON COULTHARD LTD. If they're lucky they'll have been able to swerve around a 14-wheel Hayton Coulthard pantechnicon thundering down one of the narrow approach roads. There's little doubt about which is the most important family in these parts.

The business was founded in 1916 by David's great grandfather. It passed through four generations to David's father, and then to his children. David's brother, Duncan, three years his senior, is the firm's managing director. Lynsay works there too. Both still live in Twynholm, as do their parents when they are not spending time at their second home in La Manga, Spain.

David was different. Not for him the security of close family and friends in a familiar, stable environment. His path held a little more pizzazz. 'It was his father's fault,' jokes one family friend. 'All three of the kids had motorbikes to play on in the land behind the house and Duncan bought David his first kart. Duncan was

When DC was 11 his father Duncan bought him this very kart, his first. Despite an initial reluctance, David soon discovered he had huge natural talent for the sport that would come to dominate his life. (Courtesy of the David Coulthard Museum)

David travelled with his family to karting events across the country and throughout Europe. He was serious about his sport from a very young age, and woe betide anyone who stopped him getting his beauty sleep the night before a race! (Courtesy of the David Coulthard Museum)

More silverware. The picture is a little grainy, but it doesn't hide the fact that DC looks very cool for a 12-year-old. The immaculate velvet crush suit is straight out of *Saturday Night Fever*. (Courtesy of the David Coulthard Museum)

mad about motor racing, but he was never able to do it professionally. I think he got a lot of his frustration and ambition out through David.'

By the standards of some of his contemporaries, David's introduction to the noisy, smelly, exciting world of kart racing was late – many junior karters begin to practise their skills aged four or five. Tardy though he was, the intensity of his application to this new adventure set him apart. From the start he wanted to know how the kart worked, what would make it go faster, how best to prepare for the differing demands of the tracks he would race on, like Stranraer, Larkhall near Glasgow, and Rowrah in Cumbria. Karting provided him with the ideal arena in which to indulge his compulsion to improve his environment. Speak to any David Coulthard acquaintance and not one will have missed his fastidiousness, his perfectionist streak.

'He was always cleaning his kart and playing with it,' says Lynsay. 'He would wax and polish it for days after each event. I started kart racing as well, a few years after David, and I could never be bothered to clean my kart or the kit. My race suits would go straight into the bag after a race and they'd not look so good a week later. But not David. His would be out as soon as he got home and he'd be polishing and waxing down the

leathers. For a while we even shared a helmet, so we'd only have the one between us at some events. Sometimes I would finish my race and I'd have to sprint over and give it to him so's he could start. It was our very first helmet. He never said he minded sharing it, but I'm not so sure.'

Success came fast: in only his second year of karting, 1983, David won the coveted Scottish Junior Kart Championship – an achievement he repeated in 1984 and 1985. The sport quickly began to dominate his life and that of his family. At home, mum, dad, Duncan and Lynsay started to notice odd new habits in David's behaviour. He would go missing from time to time, without having told anyone where they could find him. Lynsay soon learned to look for him in the downstairs pool room, where her brother would be lying silently on the pool table, his head held out over one end. 'He knew that you had to have a strong neck in motor racing, especially if you wanted to progress, so he'd lie there with his head out, making the muscles work. He'd stay there for ages.'

They would travel to events *en famille* in a motorhome bought by Duncan. 'Coulthards Racing Team' was written in a Germanic script down its flanks. They would travel to circuits such as Larkhall, 60 or so

DC's assault on Formula Ford was a very slick affair: he had prepared all winter for the step up to single-seaters and his Van Diemen was well backed. He won 22 of 28 races in 1989. (Courtesy of the David Coulthard Museum)

David looks pretty relaxed as he prepares to go into battle at Brands Hatch. His success in Formula Ford started to make people sit up and take notice. (Courtesy of the David Coulthard Museum)

miles (95km) from home. The track is less than a kilometre long and loops around in the form of a distorted boomerang. With gentle gradients at both ends it provided a tricky challenge for aspiring hot-shoes.

George Gribbin watches the youngsters come and go there today as he has since 1972. He has seen Dario and Allan, Colin and Alastair, the Smiths, the Leslies, fathers and sons... David, he says, didn't stand out from the crowd at first, although it soon became apparent that his gentle manner was something more like an exceptional calm. 'He and his father were always very organised and professional and you could see David had some speed. He was very cool and level-headed too. He wasn't one of the more excitable drivers. Just like he is in F1.'

Duncan was somewhat less detached. George remembers that along with many other fathers he would spectate from the best vantage points by offering to work as a 'pusher' (they would help get karts going again whenever they spun off and stalled). 'It's strange, but I can't seem to remember him pushing anyone but David,' says George.

Duncan and David would sometimes sneak in to Larkhall with a few other keen father-son combos.

Members of the West of Scotland Kart Club were given a key to the track with their membership, and before safety rules were tightened in recent years they were entitled to practise whenever they wanted. 'Practice was hardly the word for it,' says George. 'I'd come up here some afternoons and they'd be having a mini-meeting all of their own. David and Duncan would be there and the McRae boys. Maybe McNish as well. They used to say they were just getting some laps in to check their karts over. Then you would look at the lap times! It got pretty competitive.'

The atmosphere there, as at kart tracks from Sao Paolo to Stranraer, is low-key and family-orientated. Tarmac paths fray at the edges into gravel; gravel submits to grass. All the important bits are in all the right places but nothing is extra or spare. If it works, that'll do just fine. Today, a white van saying 'Gretna Flower Basket' is parked trackside. It looks out of place until the driver walks to the back doors, places a key in the lock and begins to unload tyres, fuel cans, tools, and a kart. His son, hardly tall enough to see out of the van's side windows, shadows him. He changes into his overalls and pulls on helmet and gloves. His protected head sits ludicrously large on his child's shoulders. The scent of competition hangs heavy in the air.

Few individuals here have ever been more competitive than David. On Saturday nights before the race, he would round up his family at about nine o'clock and herd them towards the motorhome, before announcing: 'Right I'm racing tomorrow, let's all be off to bed.' With that he would go. Fathers and older brothers wanting a beer with their mates were advised to socialise elsewhere. 'He took it very seriously,' says Lynsay. 'Woe betide anyone who woke him up once he'd gone to sleep.' The image of a pint-sized Coulthard bossing around mum, dad, little sis, and big bro is comical now, but from the very beginning it paid dividends in results. And his results caught eyes.

Dave Boyce was one who took notice. At the time he ran the most successful kart preparation business in Scotland; if you wanted success in karting, Boyce's number was the one to ring. He was already running one exceptionally talented young karter, Allan McNish. He had heard talk of another, called David Coulthard. He began to make discreet enquiries.

Boyce met Duncan Coulthard for the first time in Newcastle. They talked, they got on. They agreed to work together to take David as far as they could. The first year he remembers as 'fairly fraught, with the usual slips and spins'. But by '85 David was becoming the man to beat. 'It all happened very quickly,' Boyce says. 'We started just by doing a bit of work together and then all of a sudden we were away every weekend. There were little disasters and the usual slips and fallings-off you always get. But by '85, '86, '87 he became very dominant in junior karting.'

David had been helped hugely in his early exploits by his father's enthusiasm and willingness to dig deep into the coffers. But it was far from being a big-budget operation. 'It's not like some of these kids and their dads now who think they can just buy their way to Formula 1,' recalls Boyce. 'We worked really hard, you know. It seemed like we were never off the M6, slogging up and down. We certainly didn't throw money at it.' What they did throw at it was time – as

much as they could and then some. After a weekend's racing they would have to pack up the karts and equipment and gear and begin the haul back home. If they had been racing abroad that meant driving through the night, with David sleeping in the motorhome. 'There were plenty of times when we had to pretty much drop him off at the school gates from the motorhome. He'd hop off, say goodbye, and go straight into class. It took a massive effort from his parents: Duncan was still running the business full time at that stage.'

School for David was Kirkudbright Academy, five miles or so from home. In its heavy granite walls are built Scottish values of probity, solidity, propriety. David's admission that his favourite subject was 'bike shed biology' seems at odds with the stern seriousness of the place.

By his mid-teens racing had become more of a focus than had his education. After leaving the Academy, he went on to begin a business studies course, but, as his sister puts it, 'He was asked to decide whether he wanted to concentrate on his racing or on his college work. It wasn't really much of a choice. Who knows, he could have been managing Safeway in Kirkcudbright by now...' Fate was pulling him along. So competitive was the faster Super 1 kart category David had graduated to by 1987 that it demanded all his attention. Formal education would have to be put on hold.

By now he had developed a close working and personal relationship with Dave Boyce, who was revelling in having found a second karter to match the talents of his first protégé, McNish. 'David pretty much followed on where Allan left off with me,' he says, 'and it was fascinating to compare them. Allan was the sort of guy you couldn't keep off the kart. He wanted to be on the track all the time, whatever we were working on. As long as it had a steering wheel and would respond to his input, he'd just get in and do it. David was more meticulous. If we changed anything on his kart he

The start of something big: David was recruited to join Paul Stewart Racing for 1990. Clockwise from left are: Gil de Ferran, Paul Stewart, Jackie Stewart, Derek Higgins, and DC. (Courtesy of the David Coulthard Museum)

David gets a few last-minute tips from Dad before the Spa F3000 race in 1992: 'Now look, it doesn't matter where you start, you're better than the lot of 'em!' (Courtesy of the David Coulthard Museum)

wanted to know what we had changed and why. While Allan could win races against the odds, David wanted everything to be perfect. David's approach was the sort that would bring you a championship.' It did, three more times, in karts: in '86 he was Scottish open champion and in '87, British Super 1 Champion. He took the Scottish open title again in '88.

The record books tell nothing of the dedication behind the scenes. David was tall for his age and with his height came extra weight. Karts weigh little more than 100 kilos (220lb) including the driver, so any extra pounds behind the wheel would immediately show in slower lap times. 'David was always worried about his weight,' says Boyce, 'because he was on the upper limit for his category. But even there he showed his dedication. He wouldn't eat sweets and crisps, or any of the stuff that most 15-year-olds like. He knew it would get in the way of what he wanted.'

There had been further hurdles to success. Over the winter of 1986/7, for example, Boyce had decided to switch from the widely used and successful Wright karts to the untried Zip karts, built by his friend Martin Hines. 'People thought we were mad,' he says, 'but we

reckoned we had enough time to develop them.'

It was a challenge for a young driver to be sufficiently objective and analytical to compare one chassis with another and suggest where improvements should be made. David could have been tailor-made for the task. 'We spent the whole winter working away,' says Boyce. 'It was brilliant fun. His dedication and ability to get through the work really brought us the title in '87. He drove pretty well, too!' Well enough, in fact, to take wins at both of the rain-hit rounds in the 1987 championship. Each win was taken under pressure as they were vital for his championship ambitions. David was equal to the task.

By the end of that year his talent was becoming increasingly clear. 'We could all tell that here was someone a bit special,' says Boyce. 'At tracks like Larkhall and Stranraer he was exceptional. The attitude and ambition were obvious. He also knew he had to work and that it wouldn't be enough to buy his way into F1 like some of the kids try to do now.'

The '80s were a golden era for Boyce, with both McNish and Coulthard passing through his hands. They raced against each other for only one season, '85, but

This is David's Van Diemen RF89 Formula Ford, which he drove with such success in 1989. It, too, is kept in the David Coulthard Museum, where the exhibits include the results sheet from 1989, showing '1st' all the way down.

Several of David's winning cars are kept at the David Coulthard Museum in his home town of Twynholm. His Formula 3 car from 1991 is in the foreground; behind is his 1993 Pacific Reynard-Cosworth.

they became – and remain – good friends. One fond McNish memory is of a trip to Blackpool with the Coulthard family after Allan had broken his leg in a karting accident in '84. 'I had a massive plaster cast on,' he says, 'which wasn't really ideal for the fairground rides. David wanted to get us on the loop-the-loop and I said "there's no way I'll get on. I'm too short to make the minimum height." Somehow we got on and I ended up sitting in the car, rattling around because I was too small to reach the harness, and my leg whacked against the side. It broke the plaster cast and messed my leg around. I had to go back to hospital and have it all re-set. It put me back three months. I'm still not sure if David got me on there deliberately…'

David's sister would likely sympathise with McNish's suspicions. As children and young teenagers they often went together on family holidays to Barbados. Jet-skis were David's favourite diversion and every day he would head off into the Caribbean with Lynsay on the back seat. She still has the bruises to show for it: 'It

was always top speed, as you might expect, and I'd be hanging on for dear life. Then he used to stand the thing on its nose and throw me off. We would always be going at such a speed that I'd hit the water really hard and my life vest would come off. So I'd be there, bobbing about in the sea, hurting, and David would circle me, saying "Do you want to get back on, do you want to get back on?" and laughing. He'd leave me there for 20 minutes sometimes. I was never safe anywhere near the pool either. He would just appear from nowhere and rugby-tackle me straight into the water. It was typical older brother stuff, I suppose.'

Typical, except that David was anything but. 'I shouted to him in the shower once, through the bathroom door, "So are you going to be a Formula 1 driver then?" He shouted back, "Of course I am, and I'm going to work as hard as I can to get there." I was a little bit upset because I thought it meant I'd never see him again. But then, when I got used to the idea, I thought it was pretty cool.'

Champagne tastes all the sweeter when you've won: this is Portugal 1995, David's first F1 win. It would be more than a year before he stood on the top step again.

drive
my car

When David settled down to pack his suitcase for the 1994 Canadian Grand Prix (a task he has always performed with immaculate precision) he would have been well advised to include a copy of Machiavelli's *The Prince* for a little light reading as he crossed the Atlantic. Its pages might have helped him understand the powerful, unpredictable forces at work behind the scenes, shaping his career, dictating his future. One of these was the politically-charged Renault Formula 1 operation, Renault Sport, led by Christian Contzen.

Contzen, a marketing man by training, was a highly influential figure within the Williams-Renault partnership. As the general manager of the company which supplied Williams with the best engines in F1, his opinions had to be acknowledged by Frank Williams and the team's technical director Patrick Head. When Ayrton Senna was killed, Contzen had been one of the first to insist that Williams replace him with another 'ace'. While he had been impressed by David's performance at the Spanish Grand Prix, and enjoyed a good relationship with him, Contzen did not yet believe David sufficiently experienced to help carry the team at such a traumatic time. David would do, he said, for a race or two, but he was not 'The Answer'. That answer, as far as Contzen was concerned, was 41 years old, lived in a beach house in Clearwater, Florida, and was called Nigel.

Nigel Ernest Mansell had won a championship in a Renault-powered Williams in '92, and, so Contzen believed, he could be the man to do it again – or at least assist Damon Hill to do so. Alain Prost, the only other

putative candidate for the job, was also an ex-Williams-Renault World Champion. He had won that title – his fourth – in '93, but had retired at the end of the season and was emphatic that he did not want to drive in Formula 1 again. Thus only Mansell, in Contzen's eyes, had the blend of speed and experience necessary to be considered any kind of Senna 'replacement'.

Williams's commercial director Richard West was dispatched to Florida to lure him back. He remembers the period vividly: 'There was a very strong feeling at Renault at that moment that perhaps they should withdraw from F1. In their international dealer network, the feeling was, "My God, we cannot be associated with this". There were some very dark times after Ayrton's accident. We had to work hard to talk them around. Between Monaco and the Spanish Grand Prix discussions were had between Frank Williams, Renault, Rothmans and Bernie Ecclestone about Nigel coming back. David got the drive for Spain, but in the gap between there and the Canadian Grand Prix, Frank said to me: "Richard, I'm intending to bring Nigel Mansell back. I may need you to negotiate on my behalf."'

West took British Airways flight 293 to Miami on 1 June 1994, along with Duncan Mayell, Williams's financial director, and Peter Goodman from Williams's lawyers, Pickworths. 'When we arrived at Tampa airport,' says West, 'there was no messing around with hire cars or taxis. Nigel picked us up himself in this huge, red Bentley convertible. We were in stitches because on the plane we'd been wondering whether or not he would pick us up, and there he was, as we stepped off the plane,

33

Renault's Christian Contzen was a fan of David but pushed hard for Mansell's return. His background in Renault's marketing department had convinced him of the need for a 'superstar' in a front-running F1 team.

David had done enough on his F1 debut to get a second race at the 1994 Canadian GP, where he got the drop on team-mate Hill at the start. Fast starts had been a Coulthard trademark since junior racing days.

arguing with a traffic cop, because he'd parked this massive red car in a no parking zone. It was comical really, being picked up by a World Champion, who was about to get a parking ticket, but the whole thing was very Nigel.'

West's diary entry for 2 June reads as follows: 'Had a full day of discussions and had difficulty on a number of points. These points were later resolved following discussions with Frank Williams and Bernie Ecclestone.' Mansell resolved final details of his return directly with Ecclestone, via a 20-minute transatlantic telephone conversation.

An agreement had been reached under which he would race for Williams alongside Hill in four of the remaining ten grands prix. The first, in France, was three weeks away, and Mansell would then finish the season with the European Grand Prix (at Jerez in Spain), Japan, and Australia. His four-race deal would enrich him by £4 million. Damon Hill was on £500,000 for the year; David, £5,000 per race. Mansell's fee would have been healthy even by current F1 standards; in '94, it was a *very* tidy bung.

Mansell's motivations were not solely financial, however. 'I remember sitting with Nigel at Tampa on his boat, *Lionheart*,' says West. 'We just went out fishing. He said to me quietly: "I'm not undertaking this lightly, you know. I've got to go back into the team

Richard West was the man tasked with overseeing Mansell's F1 comeback. Mansell had left F1 at the end of 1992 to pursue a career in American Indycar racing, with the Newman-Haas team. He won the championship in 1993, but a less successful 1994 made him amenable to Williams's overtures. West flew to Florida to handle the negotiations face-to-face, his persuasive powers and an open chequebook being enough to convince Mansell.

where one of the greatest drivers in the world lost his life." He knew what the team had been through and what he would have to try to bring them. The feeling at Williams was that Nigel coming back brought back some gravitas. He was someone who had raced so hard with Ayrton and he commanded massive respect and that really helped lift people's spirits.

'DC was obviously somewhat disappointed, but he was also very gracious when he realised the enormity of what had been handed to him. He accepted that the team needed someone of Nigel's stature to give them a lift at that time. Losing Ayrton had been almost a mortifying blow. The pressure on the team and sponsors was incredible. Nigel's stature as a World Champion and someone who was still held in high regard was invaluable at that time. Lesser drivers than DC would have thrown their toys out of the pram, but he was smart enough to realise that the team were rebuilding and that he could play a part in that.'

From Tampa, West flew to Montreal for the Canadian Grand Prix. The Mansell deal at that stage was still secret. Soon after arriving at the track he saw Ecclestone, who said to him: 'You look tired, Richard. Suntanned, but tired. That's the price of being a deal-maker.' 'I've never forgotten that,' says West, 'although I'm hardly in Bernie's league!'

Mansell's speed in a racing car had never been in question and such was his appeal to motorsport fans – in Britain at least – that he was credited with putting an extra 50,000 on the Silverstone gate for the British Grand Prix in '92. But he was also Trouble. Controversy stalked him like a shadow. Williams's technical director Patrick Head, blunt as coal, would privately remark that working with Mansell had to be experienced to be understood. 'If I told you what it was like you wouldn't believe it,' he once told a friend from another team.

Why, therefore, should Williams embrace this turbulent force at a time when calm stability was needed? Damon Hill needed support for his outside shot at the title; new boy Coulthard had enough to be thinking about without the added distraction of a media scrum surrounding a possible Mansell return. Both men's futures were under threat should Mansell come back and blow them away, as he had other team-mates in the past. Mansell-Hill or Mansell-Coulthard could make an attractive line-up for '95, should the old lion prove still quick and hungry.

Against this backdrop David Coulthard set about preparing for the '94 Canadian Grand Prix. This, the team had made it clear, was his second chance. The first, at Spain, two weeks earlier, had been compromised by the car's unreliability. But they had been impressed enough to give David another shot.

Second chances are rare in Formula 1, so perhaps that was why David, who on lap eight of the race was running ahead of Hill, was shown a large 'move over' board by his pit crew. He was driving this weekend like a man with points to prove and score. He knew that

Nigel Mansell always enjoyed huge support in Britain, but this fan, at least, felt the new generation deserved a chance. His wish was fulfilled – although not straight away.

the best way to show the team he was worth his seat was by matching or beating Hill, and at the start the whippersnapper got the drop on his team leader, moving up from fifth to fourth at the first corner. Ahead were the two Ferraris of Jean Alesi and Gerhard Berger, with the inevitable Michael Schumacher leading. Race two of his F1 career, and here he was, running with the big boys, showing his team leader the way to go. This was ignominious for Hill but invidious for David. He didn't want to risk angering the team by spoiling Hill's race, yet running ahead of Damon was the best possible advert for his abilities.

It soon became apparent that David was holding Hill up. Damon was 'waxing David's tail' (driving just inches from his gearbox – the sure sign of a car and driver able to go faster) and looking for a way past. Had Damon Hill been anyone other than Damon Hill at this moment, the Williams team would have been standing back in admiration of David's skilled obstinacy. As it

was, he was giving the management as much of a problem as he was Damon.

'I didn't make a good start,' Hill admitted, 'but after that I got a bit cheesed off being stuck behind David, because I was able to go quicker and I could see I was losing time. He tried to get past Berger a couple of times and I wanted to have a go too. I'll be having a word with him later.'[1] David's loss of speed had come through over-use of his tyres – 'cooking' them by using all available grip in corners and under braking. It was a short-term route to speed, as the tyres wouldn't put up with that sort of treatment for long. They soon began to lose performance – as David was finding.

Still, there was no doubt he was enjoying his first proper dice in a Formula 1 car. 'I got the better start and I felt I was entitled to race my own way. When someone is all over the back of you, you do all you can to keep him behind. Until the call came from the pits they obviously felt, as I did, that what I was

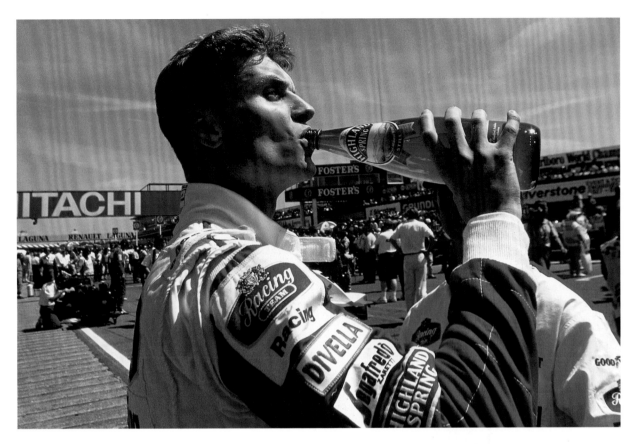

Before the start at Silverstone 1994, David was desperate to do well for the fans. He has always believed that racing in front of a home crowd is a privilege to be enjoyed to the max.

Attention to detail as always, at Spa, 1994. David led the race briefly before being called in for attention to a loose rear wing. His confidence was growing rapidly.

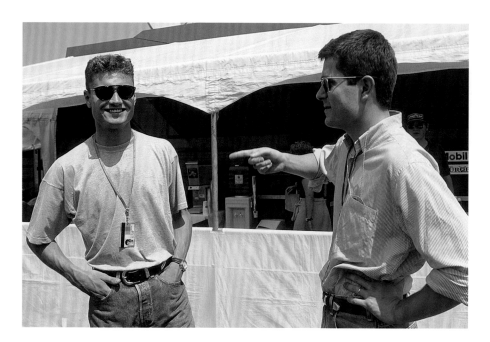

DC with friend and former rival Gil de Ferran. De Ferran reckons David is a 'bulldog' to race against, and the two had many close battles in Formula Vauxhall Lotus and Formula 3.

doing was totally justified. Eventually, on team orders, I waved him through.'[2]

It was a simultaneous blessing and curse that David should be sparring with his team-mate; blessing because he was beating the only other man on the track in the same car; curse because he was risking malodour with Williams. The only – unpleasant – alternative was to cede position. Williams solved his dilemma by issuing the pit signal.

It had been like this all weekend. In qualifying the Williams pair had traded times: on Friday afternoon David was three-hundredths of a second slower than Damon. On Saturday the times read Hill, D.: 1m 27.094s; Coulthard, D.: 1m 27.211s. Close.

Hill went on to stamp some authority on his underling by finishing the race second to Schumacher. But David's achievement in finishing fifth, for his first Formula 1 points, was also impressive. It had been hard-earned, too, as an old back injury caused his right foot to go numb. At one stage he was having to use his left foot to push his right foot down onto the brake pedal.

So much for the pins and needles. What about the pins he should have been inserting into his Nigel Mansell voodoo doll? It seems David might have overlooked that detail amid the euphoria of his first F1 score, for barely

had the teams returned to Europe from North America, than 'Our Nige' was once again all across the back pages: his four-race deal had been made public. David was sanguine. With a resolutely upbeat outlook that would become his trademark, he observed: 'Look, I started the year in F3000. Now I've driven in my first two grands prix and scored points. I knew I was signing a race-by-race contract, so I'm not surprised that Nigel is coming back. I'll still be testing for the team.'

From the minute Mansell parked his backside in FW16 chassis number one at the French Grand Prix, it was evident he intended to prove he was worth every shilling of his £1m-per-race deal. In Friday practice Mansell felt his way around the Magny-Cours circuit, telling the team (as had Senna, Hill, and Coulthard) that the car's back end was 'loose', that it wanted to break away and spin the car round when a driver turned into a corner. This uncomfortable truth was what the team wanted confirmed. But only after hearing it from a man whose driving expertise they did not question, could they fully accept that the opinions of their two current, more junior, drivers were not wayward. With Senna gone, they needed Mansell as a benchmark. More than that, Williams needed his ability to 'go out and give it one' to be certain the car was being driven to its maximum. Mansell in full flight wasn't always pretty to watch, but, oh boy, did it hold your attention.

The qualifying hour on Saturday afternoon was the arena for a classic piece of Mansell showbiz. It was a breathless session, during which he set a time good enough for pole position, for most of the 60 minutes. With the lap done, he stepped out of 'his' FW16, and was treated to a very public display of back-slapping bonhomie from Christian Contzen; Mansell's performance had been the perfect endorsement of his efforts to get the '92 World Champion back into the team.

As the qualifying hour drew to a close, Damon Hill remained in his garage, in his cockpit, ready to attempt another 'flier'. He was doubtless piqued by the endless Renault corporate glad-handing going on around Mansell, and as he pulled out of the pits his famous, fierce eyebrows were knitted tight.

Hill had been Mansell's closest rival throughout practice and he was about to find it within himself to take his FW16 to a new limit. At the end of his final qualifying lap, he came out of the last corner completely 'crossed up', power hard on, rear tyres smoking, and tail snaking away from him as driver and chassis tried to contain a surfeit of power and cornering speed. It was spectacular and effective. Hill shaved seven-hundredths of a second from Mansell's time.

Critics noted that this was a car Hill had been driving all year, one which Mansell had driven competitively for the first time 24 hours ago. But still Damon had seemed motivated into digging deeper than ever before. He would never admit that was the case. He felt his driving had said everything, as he felt it did again when he finished second (to Schumacher) on Sunday.

Mansell, who had been running a distant third, retired on lap 45. His return had been dramatic but inconclusive. The scoreboard showed *nul points* for Mansell, N.; the sweat and red face betrayed how hard he was working to find his speed. Frank Williams, however, was convinced: 'He was worth every penny, we still want him for the last three races.' But the observant recalled Williams's comment on Mansell shortly after Senna was signed for '94: 'He did not figure in our plans at all. He's over there in another category of racing which suits him and we're over

here.'[3] As for David… he found it hard to contain his enthusiasm at Mansell's retirement.

There was just a week now before the British Grand Prix at Silverstone. David would be back in the Williams, as Mansell had to return to America for the Indycar round at Cleveland, Ohio. He had endured an uncomfortable ten days watching an old pro enjoy the first instalment of an extended last hurrah – and at his expense. Once again David would be getting into an F1 car with a point to prove.

Even by Formula 1's (double) standards, the intrigue surrounding the occupants of the two Williams cars was dark and deep. Against all expectations it was now Hill under pressure. The British media's interpretation of events in France was to confirm that Mansell was, indeed, the man Williams should employ for 1995 as their lead driver, with emerging superstar Coulthard as his number two. Hill? Well, look how hard he had to work to keep that old man Mansell back in qualifying. In a further twist, Ferrari's Jean Alesi was being touted as a possible Williams driver for '95, Frank Williams long having been a fan of his cockpit heroics.

When the F1 troupe rolled into the Silverstone paddock on the Thursday before the race, they found Damon in a belligerent mood. He blasted the assembled British press for calling into question his position within the team, pointing to the fact that he was the only driver giving any kind of a fight to Schumacher and that he had just, in case they had forgotten already, beaten Nigel Mansell to pole position in France (as he had Alain Prost a year earlier). 'All that I'm reading in the papers is that my job is in jeopardy. It is not!' (Hill was right as far as his immediate future went, but he may have had cause to regret those words when he was sacked by Williams, in mid-'96, to make way for Heinz-Harald Frentzen.) Rant over, Hill was majestic thereafter, taking pole position (by three-thousandths of a second, from Schumacher), fastest lap, and the race win.

David's weekend was less polished. He qualified seventh, but stalled on the grid and caused the first 'start' to be aborted. He took the restart from the back of the grid, charged, spun, charged again up to fifth, but with his car stuck in top gear towards the end of the race and with interference from a local taxi firm coming through on his pits-to-car radio, had to settle for a lapped sixth (which later became fifth after Schumacher was disqualified for ignoring a black flag).

It had been a less-than-perfect British Grand Prix, and David knew it. 'When you get to F1 you want to do it all straight away. I don't want to appear ungrateful for the situation; it's just that I realise I have to perform well. If I don't, I'm out.'[4] But he wouldn't be out for the next five races, barring disaster. His 'race-by-race' contract with Williams had him alongside Hill for the German, Hungarian, Belgian, Italian, and Portuguese grands prix. This was as much security as David had ever known in Formula 1 and it was about to pay dividends.

Germany, though, was a missed opportunity. He took sixth place in practice and his race was brought to a premature halt when his car once again became stuck in sixth gear. He had earlier suffered a 'totally unacceptable' nose-bending tap from future McLaren team-mate, Mika Häkkinen, which necessitated a quick

fix in the pits. Frustrating, for David and the team, after he had taken the car to fastest race lap – a new record of 1m 46.211s.

Hungary, two weeks later, was pointless again, although David was unlucky to miss a podium finish. He had qualified third behind Schumacher and Hill and was running third with 18 laps to go when he spun on oil dropped on the track by Jean Alesi's Ferrari. He crashed heavily and was lucky not to be injured.

David had driven five grands prix and scored four points from two fifth places. Mechanical problems had hampered his efforts at three of those races, but he was in need of a less lean result, or at least a performance which would show he could run right at the front. Even at such an early point in his F1 career, he was entering that delicate stage where reputations are made and opinions formed. In a front-running team like Williams there was nowhere to hide. A couple of fifths were okay for a newbie finding his feet, but for a youngster being touted as a new British hero and with a race-winning car to drive, more was now expected.

Jock Clear, David's Williams race engineer, reckons Coulthard has an inner 'Incredible Hulk' which he is unable to control, and that this rage can inspire him to greatness.

At the 1994 Portuguese GP, David proved himself a winner in waiting, but had to resign himself to following home team leader Hill in support of Damon's title bid.

The next opportunity to shine would be at the Belgian Grand Prix. 'I went there feeling a bit down,' he recalls, 'because I had not had the results I had hoped for. But as soon as I got to the track I was very, very quick in wet conditions'.[5]

The Spa-Francorchamps circuit was the ideal place at which to seal or salvage a reputation. Viewed from above, it's a loop of spaghetti dropped onto the Ardennes hills, its squiggles and whirls left as they fell. Challenging. Daunting. A place where the good do well and the greats etch themselves into the pages of motor racing history. Aficionados like to call it a 'driver's circuit', a track where talent can make up for mechanical shortcomings. Juan Manuel Fangio won here, as had past champions Giuseppe Farina, Alberto Ascari, Jack Brabham, Phil Hill, Jim Clark, John Surtees, Jackie Stewart, Emerson Fittipaldi, Niki Lauda, Mario Andretti, Jody Scheckter, Alain Prost, Ayrton Senna, and Nigel Mansell. This year, Michael Schumacher, runaway leader of the '94 World Championship, was expected to win. He had brilliantly qualified seventh at

Spa on his Formula 1 debut in '91, won there – his first victory – a year later, and in '93 finished second.

In '94, the script was a little different. Pole position went to David's old Formula 3 rival, Rubens Barrichello, driving a Jordan. The track had been wet in practice, but Barrichello ran his car with slick tyres, rather than the grooved versions designed for wet conditions. The gamble was inspired; Rubens's talent and feel did the rest. David wanted to take a similar chance, but was unable to pit and change his tyres before the end of the session. He lined up seventh, but by lap three of the race was up to third, behind Hill. Both changed tyres, Hill on lap 12 and Coulthard on 13, and after the stops David emerged in front. He looked silken in second, running comfortably ahead of his team leader and emerging as a possible threat to Schumacher. When Michael made his second stop on lap 28 David actually led a grand prix for the first time. Now the CV was starting to look a little better. Race six: led lap 29.

Yet again, however, a technical problem was about to intervene. His car's rear wing was visibly wobbling and

he was called into the pits on lap 37 for it to be checked over. Technical director Patrick scowled his way around the back of the car, before declaring it fit to race and sending David back out again. He finished fifth, despite intermittent gearbox problems late in the day. Hill finished second. Schumacher, who finished first on the road, was later disqualified for a technical infringement, gifting Hill the win and elevating David to fourth. A certain podium, possibly even his first win – in his sixth Formula 1 race – had slipped through his fingers.

Schumacher's no-score had a profound effect on the course of the '94 championship. Hill's ten points for his 'bonus' win hauled him back to within 21 points of Schumacher, and his bitter rival was about to miss the next two races. Schumacher's penalty for his transgression in ignoring the black flag at Silverstone was a two-race ban. His Benetton team opted to 'rest' Michael for the Italian and Portuguese Grands Prix. For Hill this was a double open goal with no opposition keeper. In a car better than any other on the grid, he could score 20 points from both races, providing he made no errors and the Williams held together. That

being so, by the time of Michael's scheduled return at the European Grand Prix on 16 October only a point would separate them.

For David, too, this was a dream scenario. All the team were concerned about was that Damon should exploit an unforeseen opportunity. David, by supporting him, could only raise his standing at Williams, and, by extension, throughout the paddock. He understood this very clearly. Allan McNish considers David's single defining quality as a racing driver to be his ability to 'maximise his talent and maximise his opportunities'. He would do so at Monza.

Engine problems in final practice left him an unrepresentative fifth on the grid, but he had been faster than Hill on Friday and was again in the race. The Ferraris of Jean Alesi and Gerhard Berger were fastest early on, but by the end of the race, after Alesi's retirement and a slow pit stop for Berger, the Williams cars were running one-two, Hill first, David second. Hill could thank his team-mate for this, because Coulthard had come out of the pit stop sequence in the lead. His moment of glory lasted only two laps: the call came from the pits for him

The boy done good: David's first podium, alongside Damon Hill and future McLaren team-mate Mika Häkkinen. Hill could be an intense team-mate, although he and David got on well – most of the time. But there were flashpoints when Damon felt under pressure to prove his worth. By the end of 1994, DC looked to be every bit as fast as Hill.

McLaren boss Ron Dennis had spotted in David many of the qualities he admired in a driver. He went a-wooing... and ended up fighting a contractual battle with Frank Williams.

to move over and allow Hill through, to gain extra points for his championship assault.

It was galling for David to have to give away a win he could almost taste, even though he knew that was his role this weekend. A less honourable man might simply have tried to take the victory, knowing that whatever the future held, at least his name would be in the record books as a grand prix winner. It says much for David's self-confidence and racing savvy that he chose not to do so, for within a mile of the chequered flag, he ran out of fuel and slipped to sixth. Shame and opprobrium would have been heaped upon his head in equal measure had he gone for broke and run out of gas while leading, duplicitously. He could have kissed goodbye to his Williams drive too.

The result was a footnote to an impressive weekend in which he had shown himself to be a pace-setter at last. He also demonstrated he was not above playing mind games with his supposed elder and better. Hill knew that David had been instructed to pull over for him when the call came, but always there was an edge of anxiety until David actually did so. David ignored

two calls from the pits before letting Hill past – just enough of a delay to let Damon know he was no pushover, without upsetting his paymasters.

Drivers and team left Monza content. Hill had won; David knew he could have won; the championship campaign was still on course. David was walking tall, confidence higher than ever. It showed in the intensity of his manner away from the track. His race engineer at Williams, Jock Clear, recalls his surprise at the hard edge to relations between David and Damon: 'It seems almost crazy when I think of it now, but I remember once Damon sitting in the motorhome having a cup of tea and a Twix. He had eaten one finger and the second one was sitting in the wrapper. David came by and picked it up for a laugh. Damon, being deadly serious, grabbed David and held his hand so tight he almost broke David's finger. The laughter stopped pretty quickly I can tell you. They weren't messing around. They very nearly came to blows. DC was on the point of saying "Right, outside now" in a very broad Scottish accent. It was incredibly intense between them sometimes.'

Damon's brooding surliness was often apparent, but

The tug of love between Frank Williams and Ron Dennis for David's services never became hostile, but DC found himself both flattered and bemused by the attention he was attracting at such an early stage in his career.

with David, the capacity for anger came as more of a surprise. 'It's something over which he has no control,' says Clear. 'It's a sudden aggressive streak almost like the Incredible Hulk. He can't bring it on himself and he can't suppress it when it rises. It's not necessarily something that's made him angry that triggers it. It can be something that's nibbling away inside and it will bubble up and it can be really quite impressive when it does. When he has it in the car and he channels it, he's absolutely unstoppable.'

As he was about to be at the Portuguese Grand Prix, where David proved what the world already knew: he was a winner in waiting. From third on the grid, he sped past Hill to chase Gerhard Berger's Ferrari, which had started from pole position. Once again David was showing genuine, front-running pace in one of the two fastest cars on the track. Berger was slightly holding up the Williams pair and David started to sniff for a way past. He didn't have to: on lap seven the Ferrari pulled off with broken transmission. Not that David felt he needed the Ferrari to expire to take the lead: 'Berger was already getting a bit ragged,' he said later, 'and I think I could probably have pressured him into some sort of mistake.'[6] Coulthard: eight grands prix; Berger: an established 'ace' in his tenth F1 season. This was a young man on the crest of a wave. He led in dominant style for the next 10 laps and emerged from the first series of pit stops still ahead. Once again he knew team orders would be brought into play, should the need arise, but there was a feeling here of a young man enjoying his place in the sun.

Hill eventually went past David on lap 27 and together they cruised one-two to the flag, putting on a staged finish to cross the line a second apart. This was the first Formula 1 one-two for two British drivers since Damon's father Graham Hill finished ahead of Piers Courage at the '69 Monaco Grand Prix.

It had been an immaculate day for Williams, with Hill now on 75 points to Schumacher's 76, prior to his return at the next round, the European Grand Prix at Jerez. And David, who would have to sit out the final three rounds and watch Nigel Mansell take his drive, would leave the sport – temporarily – with the image of his grinning, clean cut features beaming from the second step of the podium. He had achieved the perfect second place, if such a thing is possible. *Autosport*, the British weekly motorsport 'bible', was in no doubt about the scale of his achievement. In tones redolent of a Pathé news dispatch circa 1943, it opined: 'The writing is on the wall. The Williams-Renault team should sign David Coulthard immediately to join Damon Hill in its line-up for '95. Their one-two was … clear evidence that Williams does not need Nigel Mansell for next season, or even for the remainder of this.' 'Huzzah!', one might almost have added.

It was hard to disagree with the sentiment. David's stock was high and rising. He had received offers from other teams to drive for them in the last three races, and he indicated his keenness not to have to sit on the sidelines when his form was so strong. Williams, however, had written a clause into his contract preventing him from driving for a team whose performance might compromise Hill's title challenge. A team such as Benetton, for example, or McLaren, whose principal Ron Dennis had spotted in David the qualities of speed, presentation, and all-round professionalism which he valued highly. Highly enough, indeed, to invite David for dinner at the next race, in Jerez. This was the first race for which the Nigel Mansell charabanc was back in town, but rather than stay away David had committed to travelling to the last three grands prix of the year, as much to niggle Nigel as anything else.

Without a car to race David found himself with time to kill in the evenings and he was delighted, therefore, to accept Dennis's dinner invitation. They ate together at the circuit restaurant in the Quaver Park Hotel. The talk was light and upbeat, but within a framework – Ron Dennis doesn't 'do' casual. He was sounding David out and extolling the virtues of McLaren's newly announced five-year engine partnership with Mercedes Benz. It emerged a little later that following the dinner, David had, in fact, signed a letter of intent with McLaren for the '96 season. He had taken advice from his manager, Tim Wright of IMG, the leading sport management agency, and was now, effectively, on the books of two teams, Williams also having an option on David's services for '95.

The rationale was clear to see. David's position at Williams was still unclear (although Mansell's finishing in the gravel at Jerez did David no harm whatsoever), so if Ron Dennis had expressed an interest, well, it would have been rude not to respond in kind, wouldn't it? In interviews David tried to laugh off the interest surrounding his future, as he did his frustration at Mansell's return: 'I think my helmet blends into the Williams colour scheme much better.' But the issue wouldn't go away. With Hill and Schumacher heading for a showdown at the last race of the season, the Australian Grand Prix, David (unbeknown to him) was heading for the courts, as Williams sought to establish his precise contractual position. And Mansell, of course, was about to steal the show, the headlines, and everyone else's thunder by winning in Adelaide and putting himself right back in contention for the second Williams drive.

Hill and Schumacher had clashed on lap 36, putting both out of the race and allowing Mansell through for his 31st grand prix win. All David's toil and dutiful understudying suddenly looked likely to be negated by a trademark Mansell showstopper. Amid the post-race furore, Williams stated publicly that Hill had been re-signed for '95, but no announcement was made about his team-mate, leaving David and Mansell as rivals for the same seat.

The F1 media couldn't get enough of this, and as David kept his head beneath the parapet, on holiday in the Far East, Ron Dennis expertly stoked the fires by

McLaren's Jo Ramirez, Coulthard ally and confirmed fan. He took the call from David's manager, Tim Wright, who 'did a pretty good sales job' for DC.

admitting to his interest in Coulthard. 'Of the young drivers, Barrichello, Häkkinen and Coulthard have the most potential. Coulthard has driven some exceptional races, but he has had a competitive package. I think he's a great talent.'[7] Dennis was also, genuinely, on the look out for a partner to his still-raw speed merchant, Mika Häkkinen. Neither Martin Brundle, nor Philippe Alliot, both of whom drove for McLaren alongside Mika in '94, were deemed worthy of a '95 drive. David's prospects of a seat there looked rosier. Woking, in Surrey, where the team were based, seemed a sensible destination for him. His first ever run in a Formula 1 car had been in a McLaren, in '91, as part of his reward for being named McLaren/*Autosport* Young Driver of the Year.

There was the further inducement of a £500,000 per season contract from McLaren for '96 – an offer made in the strictest confidence to Coulthard and manager Tim Wright. It looked particularly attractive at a time when Williams were paying only £5,000 per race and

offering no guaranteed tenure for the following season. David's management were strongly in favour of his accepting the deal, even if it would mean sacrificing Williams's performance advantage over their rivals, at least in the short-term. McLaren, they believed, would not be down for long.

Jo Ramirez, then McLaren team co-ordinator and close confidante of Ron Dennis, remembers the first time David's name was mentioned seriously in connection with a McLaren drive. 'I was working late at the factory in Woking one night when the phone rang. It was a pleasant-sounding man who said his name was Tim Wright and that he was David Coulthard's manager. He wanted to speak to Ron, but he wasn't there, so we got talking. I had known DC a bit since he came to F1 that year with Williams and I met him first, briefly, when he won his young driver award. That was actually when we started looking at him as a driver.

'Tim Wright was very persuasive you know, about David, saying what a good young talent he was and

how he could fit in well at McLaren. DC was doing well at Williams and Tim Wright was doing a very good PR job for him, I must say! The next day I went and spoke to Ron and said that definitely here was a guy who was going to go places. We had noticed that as well as being a good driver he was also very good at personal PR. He spoke well and presented himself very well. I started to get to know David better that year, especially when we were fighting over him with Williams.'

As David was topping up his tan, Williams were instructing George Carman QC, one of the country's leading barristers, to represent them at Formula 1's contracts recognition board in Geneva. This independent body of three lawyers specialising in contract law, sat to decide on disputes between teams over drivers. David's was the most high profile yet, as they had to establish whether a letter of intent between McLaren and David for '96 could come between Williams and David in '95. It took them ten days to announce their decision: that, for '95, 'Williams

are the team entitled to the services of David Coulthard'. Even then it was not until 2 January 1995 that David was finally confirmed as a Williams race driver for the season ahead.

The British press had been desperate to find out whether Williams had chosen Mansell or Coulthard. One paper ran a story confirming Coulthard, before the announcement was made. Team press officer Ann Bradshaw later asked the journalist how he had been confident enough to run the story, when all at Williams were sworn to secrecy. 'He told me it was obvious because I was happy when he rang me to try to find out. He said if it had been Nigel I would have been much more gloomy.'

When the dust settled it became clear that money had been the motivation behind the initial talks with McLaren. Many believed the whole affair had been engineered and inflated simply to get David a pay rise at Williams (his 16-race '95 contract was worth £500,000). Be that as it may, Ron Dennis's interest in David was genuine – as it should have been after David's remarkable first half-season. In just eight races he had gone from broke F3000 driver, to F1 team tester, to Senna replacement, to race leader, to Mansell rival, to central character in Williams-DC-McLaren love triangle, to full-time Williams-Renault F1 driver. Amid a degree of sniping that David had been lucky – in the right place at the right time – many overlooked the fact that he had made one of the most high-profile, high-pressure Formula 1 debuts ever. And he hadn't messed up.

'In the car is the only time in your very public life that you have the privilege to do what you love doing. No one is there disturbing you.'[8]

David Coulthard had never been loud. He never courted celebrity. He was becoming a public figure because of his talent in a racing car and he understood that being a leading Formula 1 driver meant he had relationships with his team, their sponsors, and the media, all of which had to be nurtured and maintained.

The sentiments he expressed on the eve of his first full racing season were unchanged more than eight years later, as he prepared for the 2003 Monaco Grand Prix: 'I don't walk around thinking about racing. Even after all these years I'm still slightly embarrassed when people recognise me. I like to race and then I like to go home and that is why I am never going to inspire the masses. To me, all the things around the paddock can be a distraction. I just like going home and feeling like I've had a good day in the office.' He was a racing driver, pure and simple. The rest he could take or leave. All he wanted was to be judged on his own terms – on his good and bad days in the office.

In '95 there would be plenty of both. That year's Williams, the FW17, was a step on from its originally wayward predecessor. The team had known for months that they would have to share their coveted Renault engines with Michael Schumacher's Benetton team, so an even tougher fight for the championship was expected than in '94, when the spoils were shared: Schumacher took the drivers' title for his team; Williams won constructors' honours. Technical director Patrick Head and chief designer Adrian Newey, Formula 1's foremost aerodynamics specialist, had worked hard to ensure that the Williams side of the Williams-Renault partnership was top notch.

The intra-team battle would likely be tough, too, as Hill and Coulthard had proved particularly closely matched towards the end of '94. At the car's launch Head noted: 'I certainly don't think any other team has a stronger driver pairing but I think undoubtedly there will be conflict and if there isn't I shall be disappointed.' Williams made it very clear that no team orders would be imposed between their drivers. If Hill wanted to win the '95 title, he would have to beat his team-mate as well as everyone else.

The team had traditionally operated a 'tough love' school in its management of drivers, and while that made life more difficult for Hill, entering his third season with Williams and considering himself entitled to 'number one' status, it gave David a subtle psychological edge. Given his inexperience, he would not be expected to beat Damon in the championship, but neither would he be prevented from doing so.

From the first tests of FW17, both drivers were bubbling, praising the car's handling qualities, its power and comfort. They went on to prove the worth of their opinions with extremely strong early season performances. Hill took pole position at the first round, Brazil, and led convincingly until retiring with suspension failure, which allowed Schumacher to win.

David's poor form, owing to tonsillitis, led to a few forthright discussions with Frank Williams in 1995. Once recovered, however, David regained the flair which had first caught Williams's eye – but he was already McLaren-bound.

David was second. In Argentina, for round two, David took his first Formula 1 pole position at a sodden Autodromo Oscar Alfredo Galvez. The light touch he had shown throughout his career, right from his very first days in karting, was serving him well. While early pace-setter Jean Alesi, driving a Ferrari, was slip-sliding his way around the circuit, catching slides and everyone's attention with his flamboyance, David eased his way to a time eight-tenths of a second faster than anyone else's. Not only was it his first pole position, it was the first time he had out-qualified his team-mate.

He led the race from the start until it was stopped after a multiple collision on the first lap. He led again at the restart, pulling out three seconds on Schumacher, who was being chased hard by Hill. Then came trouble. An electrical problem was making the car's electronic throttle erratic and David dropped to third, behind Hill, who had made a bold pass for the lead, and Schumacher. The problem cured itself temporarily and David was able to get past Schumacher himself, but by the end of lap 16 he was out, with total electrical failure.

He was frustrated at yet another mechanical retirement, but this had been his most convincing Grand Prix weekend yet. In this car, he felt he had the measure of the two men most likely to contest the championship. So assured had been his performance, the paddock seemed to have forgotten David was in only his tenth grand prix. Like all those who belong in Formula 1, he *looked* like he belonged.

Three weeks later, at Imola, Hill took an emotional victory a year on from Ayrton Senna's death, in a Williams car. Once again David was in among the leaders, eventually finishing fourth but only after incurring the wrath of Jean Alesi for his 'incorrect' driving. He was proving to be quick and combative, a hard 'racer' as Williams are fond of describing drivers who know how to look after themselves on the track. But just like that, the Williams dream was about to go sour.

David was suffering from tonsillitis. It had struck during the off-season and then cleared up, but the pressures of international travel and the frantic nature of a grand prix driver's life had brought it back acutely. It weakened him physically and prevented him from following his usual fitness regimen. In Spain for round four, he went to bed at five o'clock each evening, in order to gain enough strength to drive the following day. He was so weakened he had discussed pulling out for a race or two, to try to recover. After taking advice from his manager and family he decided to carry on, in order to avoid developing any reputation for frailty.

Williams were lacklustre that weekend. The cars lacked grip and were unable to match the speed of the Benettons. David retired, Hill finished fourth. After four races nine points were not what he – and Williams – had been expecting. Rumours over David's position within the team began to circulate. They were dwarfed, however, by the furore surrounding Nigel Mansell's position at McLaren.

Over the '94–'95 closed-season, Mansell had signed for Ron Dennis's team when it became clear that David would be staying at Williams. His much-hyped arrival degenerated into farce when he proved to be too large to fit the cockpit of the MP4/10. For the first two races of the year, as a wider car was manufactured, his seat was filled by Mark Blundell. But by Imola, where a new, larger monocoque was ready ('you could get a stereo in there now,' Ron Dennis remarked), he was racing once more. But not for long. He finished ninth in San Marino, tenth in Spain… and by Monaco he was gone. 'Retired' was the official line. Blundell took Mansell's place for the remainder of the year and in a difficult car finished a creditable tenth in the championship. For '96, however, Dennis had other ideas about who should drive his cars. Ideas which centred around the agreement already reached between McLaren and Coulthard.

It was unfortunate for David that at the very time when he would have most wanted to impress his would-be future employers, he was enduring a run of bad form on account of his infection and his car's unreliability. Monaco and Canada were 'no-scores', despite his having qualified in third position for both races. He was back on the podium – third – in France, having undergone a tonsillectomy post-Canada, but his performance lacked some of the vigour that had come to be expected.

Silverstone, again, was disappointing. It brought another third, but David never looked more than Hill's understudy, despite battling hard with Jean Alesi. At

least he was proving a popular new arrival with British fans: 'I could hear the crowd at Copse corner cheering above the noise of the cars when I overtook him. To be able to hear that was pretty impressive.'

In Germany he went one better, but with Hill having thrown away pole position in a first corner accident, the team had wanted David to provide a stronger challenge to Schumacher, the eventual winner. Williams had opted to make only one pit stop, while Benetton chose two. Benetton's strategy proved faster and David's expected challenge failed to materialise. He said he would have pushed harder had he realised Michael was stopping twice.

It was another disappointing race, and senior Williams personnel began to talk openly about DC

being on the way out of the team. They knew of his 'private' agreement with McLaren, but they seemed keen to increase the pressure on David for as long as he remained, perhaps to improve his performances. The name most mentioned as a replacement was that of Jacques Villeneuve.

When Jacques arrived at Silverstone on 1 August, two days after the German Grand Prix, to test-drive a Williams, he was accompanied by a significant reputation. He was the son of Gilles Villeneuve, the former Ferrari idol who was killed driving for the team in practice for the '82 Belgian Grand Prix. The Villeneuve name carried great resonance for Formula 1 fans: Jacques' father had been hero-worshipped in Italy and around the world, for his seemingly possessed never-say-die style, the like of which had not been seen in grand prix racing since the days of Tazio Nuvolari in the '30s. As he arrived, Bernie Ecclestone spoke of how keen he would be to see a Villeneuve in Formula 1 again.

Jacques' credentials for a Williams race drive were strong. He had become the star driver in American Indycars and that September, aged 24, he would become the youngest ever winner of the Indycar title, America's premier category for single-seater, open-wheeled racing cars. He had also won the Indy 500 race earlier in the year (the youngest ever winner) and

was noted for his aggression at the wheel and hard-shelled composure out of the cockpit – qualities highly prized at Williams.

Creative tension is a euphemism sometimes used to describe the friction that occurs between colleagues or team-mates when they know they are having to compete for the favours of their superiors. The tension in the Williams garage that day created some fast lap times, as David, Hill, and Villeneuve finished one, two, three – none of the other teams present able to get within a second. David, in fact, was more than a second clear of Hill, but he could feel already that the mood within the team was beginning to swing against him. His frank assessment of Villeneuve's presence: 'I don't believe Williams would test him and then not have an option on him for the future, so I believe if he comes to F1 it will be with Williams. Obviously three into two doesn't go.' He was correct about Williams's option on Villeneuve: it was taken up later that month. Williams had concluded they had little option other than to sign Jacques, as they knew David was McLaren-bound.

At the next race, Hungary, Hill outshone David once again. Coulthard finished a lucky second after Schumacher's fuel pump broke on lap 73. Belgium, where David had been so strong a year earlier, was difficult too: fifth in qualifying (although ahead of Hill, in eighth) followed by a retirement. He had the consolation of having led strongly, ahead of his team-mate, until a gearbox failure.

Things were about to get a whole lot better. Italian Grand Prix: pole position; Portuguese Grand Prix: pole position; European Grand Prix: pole position; Pacific Grand Prix: pole position. Fully recovered physically, David had become Formula 1's man to beat in qualifying and had given Williams much to think about as they reflected on the talent they were losing for '96. David was showing unalloyed speed, the single quality for which a team will forgive a driver almost anything. There was also the small matter of leading, again, in Italy – although only after a spin on the warm-up lap. David was fortunate that a subsequent accident caused the race to be restarted, allowing him to set off from pole once more and lead elegantly until a lap 13 wheel bearing failure sent him into the gravel.

Leading two consecutive races had been a considerable boost to David's confidence, a subject always at the forefront of his thoughts when discussing his qualities as a driver. For the first time since Argentina, the halo of self-assurance that had dimmed and slipped during the mid-season had returned.

It had to be Portugal, where a year earlier David had eased out of the chorus line and shown that he was a driver who wanted the front of the stage. Estoril was a shoddy old track, out of keeping with the blue chip sheen of corporate-era Formula 1. The seaside town from which the circuit took its name enjoyed a frayed, paint-peely warmth which extended, incongruously, into the paddock. Still, it was a challenging track, with a pair of fast right-handers at the start of the lap and the wide open blast of Parabolica to finish.

Williams had a revised car to run this weekend. Better suspension and tweaked aerodynamics improved its performance, and while David's pole position was no surprise his margin over Hill raised eyebrows: four-tenths of a second. This was one of those weekends where something would have to go wrong to hold David back. Pole, fastest lap, and, 71 laps later, his first grand prix victory. No one else got a look in. As days in the office go, this one was pretty good.

Acknowledging the weekend as the 'high point' of his life so far, he had kind words for his team: 'The great thing is that as long as I'm not holding Damon up, then I'm free to race. Given the position in the championship [Schumacher had led Hill by 66 points to 51 before the race] you don't get fairer than that – especially as I'm leaving the team.'[9]

It had been less good for Hill, who needed the win to keep alive his chances of beating Schumacher to the '95 title. But he was a Williams driver, and he had always known never to expect favours. Besides, David had been quicker all weekend and he was genuine in his praise of his team-mate's performance. As was Frank Williams, who told one newspaper he might just have made his 'biggest mistake' in releasing David. 'He has turned into a wonderful driver,' said Williams. 'He was a brilliant winner at Estoril. We will find out next season about Jacques.'

Was it all down to the removal of a pair of tonsils? They'd have saved a bit of weight, maybe enough to gain a thousandth of a second per lap; but this was a new DC – the old DC, in fact. He had been helped, too, by a few driving tips from his old mentor, Jackie Stewart, Formula 1 World Champion in '69, '71, and '73. Just before Monza he had told David to 'brake a little earlier and a little more gently' to allow the car to carry more speed through the corners.

Receiving advice from Jackie was nothing new for David; like all of those who drove for the Paul Stewart Racing team (run by Jackie's eldest son) before F1, he benefited from 'driving lessons' from the great man. 'Most racing drivers brake late,' Stewart explains. 'Where you take them off and how you take them off is what's important. You cannot put a car into a corner in distress. Not many people understand this. Some people will tell you now that I don't understand what it's like to drive a modern Formula 1 car, but it's still true. We used to try to train the drivers up at Oulton Park in a Ford Escort world rally car. It had 450bhp so it was powerful, you know. It was always a big struggle to get drivers to let the brakes off, to convince them that they didn't have to brake as late as they did. I spent an awful lot of time doing that with our different drivers. DC had a couple of sessions there and it's something that he picked up pretty quickly. I saw the difference in his racing straight away.'

The advice certainly seemed to be working. His mental preparations had also been aided immeasurably by the knowledge that he had a team to drive for in '96; it emerged shortly before Estoril that McLaren had taken up their option on his services agreed almost a year earlier.

David was resigned to the fact that a move to McLaren would almost certainly mean a slide down the grid. They had struggled through an uncompetitive weekend at Estoril and they lacked the direction and stability of Williams. As a long-term career move, however, the value of a drive for Ron Dennis's team could not be underestimated – even if it did mean David would have to measure himself against Mika Häkkinen, now emerging as possibly the fastest driver on the grid. The deal was announced the following weekend, at the European Grand Prix, held in '95 at Germany's Nürburgring circuit. Ron Dennis, with a somewhat back-handed compliment, explained that it had been his intention to secure Coulthard since the previous November, but that he had only been able to do so once it was clear that Michael Schumacher would not be available to drive for McLaren.

David's Nürburgring weekend began well, with another pole position. He led the race, too, despite having spun on the warm-up lap and having to take over the spare car. He finished third and, lying only 12 points behind Hill, second in the championship seemed attainable.

His fifth and final pole of the season came at the Pacific Grand Prix and once again David led, for the first 48 laps, only to lose out to Schumacher during the pit stops. Michael's eighth win of the season made him champion again. The gap between Hill and Coulthard was now down to ten points and the Williams boys looked set for a bit of a shoot-out going into the last two races. But it all came to nothing. Both crashed in Japan – at the same corner, Spoon, within a lap of each other. Williams chief designer Adrian Newey said later that while the team had to take some responsibility for mechanical unreliability sacrificing results in '95, so, too, did their sometimes unreliable drivers.

Although David led at Adelaide in 1995, he went out after an embarrassing pit lane shunt. A blip in the engine management system raised the engine revs and caught DC unawares, sending him straight into the pitwall...

Which left Australia, scene of Coulthard's first great Formula 1 embarrassment. Coming in to the pits on lap 20, from the lead, he drove straight into the pit wall, breaking the car's suspension and putting him out of the race. It looked like an error of inexperience, but the bump was caused by confusion in the car's electronic 'brain', which believed the engine was about to stall and raised the revs as an emergency response. The sudden, uncontrolled increase in power caught David unawares and pushed his car into the wall. Game over.

The race had been an appropriate conclusion to a season of promise and disappointment. David's speed could no longer be questioned. Neither could his talent. And he *had* finished third in the World Championship after his first full season of Formula 1.

'You make your own decisions and you pay for the mistakes you make,' David had said at the start of the year. As he looked ahead to '96, and a challenging new life at McLaren, how prescient his words seemed.

[1] *Autosport*, 16 June 1994.

[2] Ibid.

[3] *Autosport*, 14 October 1993.

[4] *Autosport*, 14 July 1994.

[5] David Coulthard, *The Flying Scotsman* (Jim Dunn, 1995).

[6] *Autosport*, 29 September 1994.

[7] *Autosport*, 17 January 1994.

[8] *Autosport*, 19 January 1995.

[9] *Autosport*, 28 September 1995.

Who would have thought this shy teenager would become one of the leading grand prix drivers of his era? This is David preparing for a test run in his first Formula Ford car in early 1989.

with a little help from my friends

They went together, the three Davids, to Scotland's Knockhill circuit in Fife. The introductions were simple, if confusing: 'Hello David, nice to meet you. I'm David, and this is my father, David.' It was November 1988 and David Coulthard was meeting the David Leslies, father and son, for the first time.

David Leslie junior was an active and successful racing driver. With his father he had set up a racing team to bring young talent from karting into the junior levels of motor racing, in single-seat cars. In '88, for those, like DC, wishing to make the jump, that meant switching from karts to Formula Ford.

The demands of driving a full-size single-seater are different from those of a kart. There is more power but more weight. There is suspension to adjust. The machines are far bigger, with the driver fully enclosed

Soaking up the pressure at Paddock Hill bend, Brands Hatch. David's rivals had to get used to the sight of his gearbox in 1989: he dominated both the Formula Ford championships he entered.

David Leslie, who ran DC in Formula Ford in 1989 – with great success. Leslie spent the winter of 1988-9 preparing David for the season ahead, and they reaped the rewards in dominant fashion.

inside the chassis and surrounded by bodywork. Karts leave everything on top of their frame: driver, engine, and gearbox are exposed. All the circuits are different and longer. The driving sensation is less immediate. For a novice, even one who has been extremely successful in karts, single-seaters are a whole new world.

Duncan Coulthard understood his son would be faced with challenges he could not anticipate as he stepped up, and he was determined that David should spend the winter of '88 testing with an experienced Formula Ford team, to ensure he was ready for his first season outside karting. Duncan had got to know the Leslies through contacts in the racing world and in business. He was aware that they had already helped Allan McNish transfer successfully from karts to cars and he was keen to replicate that for his own son. He was prepared, also, to back his desire with hard cash and went to the Leslies with a cheque for around £10,000 in his pocket. They were impressed. Duncan

was offering talent, cash, and ambition. He would soon talk building materials supplier, Eternit, into sponsoring David's car. He also showed himself willing to listen to the Leslies' advice on how best to prepare for the season ahead. It was too good an opportunity to miss, for all involved.

'What Duncan and the family had done beforehand was to think about what they wanted to do rather than just saying "Oh, this will be all right" and trying to make the best of it,' says David Leslie junior. 'Duncan was very much involved in everything, from karting onwards, right the way up to F1. He was somebody we knew as a family friend for a period before we were racing with David. When they came to us and said they wanted to go motor racing, we told them what they would have to do.'

David's first laps were in an old Formula Ford chassis at a barren November Knockhill. He raced all of '89 in that year's latest Van Diemen RF89, but for now, a less cutting-edge machine would suffice, as he learned

David always knew how to drive in wet conditions, as he proved during the 1989 Formula Ford Festival. He went on to finish third, beaten only by more experienced drivers in the senior Formula Ford category.

Face of the future. The trademark composure would become very familiar throughout the following decade.

cornering lines and braking points. The Leslies' approach was methodical and disciplined. When David first drove around Knockhill, a track he did not know, he followed a series of cones, which showed the correct trajectory through a corner and where to aim for apex and exit. He was restricted in the amount of revs he could use at first, to prevent him getting carried away with the addictive sensation of more power and speed. 'But he learned quickly,' says Leslie. 'Once I had talked him around the track and showed him the correct line, it stuck. There was never any need to tell him twice.'

Leslie was struck also by David's intense dedication to his racing, as many others had been already. 'He would come to the workshop and he seemed to spend most of his time cleaning the car. That was something he was very good at. It was useful too, because he learned how the car worked. It didn't make him a mechanic, but it gave him a good understanding of the technical side. He was into the whole car, front to back and top to bottom. He wasn't one of the young guys who turn up for the race and then disappear. He wanted to be involved in the whole process. He wanted to get the best out of his situation and he was very good at doing that.'

David Coulthard may have been one of the best-prepared karters ever to take the grid in Formula Ford. In '89 his red and white Van Diemen contested two

championships: the Dunlop Star of Tomorrow series and the P&O Ferries Championship. Each had 14 rounds and David's main opposition came from Kelvin Burt, another talented youngster backed by a strong team, who was already a multiple Formula Ford race winner. They started the season as joint favourites, with Kelvin having the edge on account of his greater experience. David's results exceeded all expectations. He won 22 of the 28 rounds in a display of consummate dominance. A framed press release in the David Coulthard Museum shows the results hand-written onto the season's calendar. It is almost a clean sheet of '1st's, printed neatly in blue biro ink.

The first five races brought wins, in wet conditions and dry, on major British circuits: Thruxton, Brands Hatch, Silverstone, Donington. The preparation and professionalism had been important in the success, but Leslie is quick to credit David's own ability in wrapping up the season so well: 'It would be a mistake to attribute his success to the strength of the team alone. We did a good job, certainly, but a lot of it was down to DC. He still had to go out there and deliver. And he did. Even at that age he was very focused, committed, and knew what he wanted. That showed particularly when he won his first race. That took a lot of concentration and focus, especially as the track was wet. He became dominant as we know, but even when he had competition he didn't just wait and sit on his

This was a familiar view of the Coulthard Van Diemen in 1989: at the front of the pack, or impatiently chasing down the lead.

At Silverstone in 1990, David and Rubens Barrichello – a career-long rival – had put on a great show. David prevailed, although his season in Vauxhall Lotus was disappointing. Any hope of a title was ruined by a broken leg after an accident at Spa.

championship lead: he went out and fought for points and wins. He was very, very determined.'

The season could hardly have been more successful, but there was more to come. The Formula Ford year concludes with the Formula Ford Festival, an annual jamboree at Brands Hatch which draws drivers from Formula Ford championships across the world to compete in a series of heats before a final, which produces a single, outright winner. David didn't win the Festival (Brazilian Nico Palhares did), but he did finish third, behind drivers from bigger teams with more sophisticated cars.

Besides, there was a more glittering prize awaiting him several weeks later. When David arrived at London's Café Royal in January, for the increasingly prestigious awards ceremony organised by *Autosport* magazine, he regarded it as little more than a chance to put on his kilt and have a good night out. There

would be free champagne, the chance to meet a few of the sport's movers and shakers, the opportunity to build his profile. He never expected to leave that evening with the most prestigious gong of the lot: the first McLaren/*Autosport* Young Driver of the Year Award. But after the season he had put together it was little surprise to the assembled glitterati that David should be so honoured. The man himself was – uncharacteristically – lost for words. 'Did they really say my name?' he mumbled, before heading for the stage and learning that he would be given test drives in a Formula 3 car and a Formula 1 McLaren as part of his prize.

Peter Foubister, now a managing director of Haymarket Publishing, which owns *Autosport*, organised the awards as the magazine's editor. 'We had a very clear idea that we wanted to give the drivers something which would be of value to them, not only in cash terms, but also something which would improve their experience. Ron Dennis supported us from the start and in David's case he went on to reap the benefit!' (The tale has a heart-warming postscript. David wrote a letter of thanks to Peter Foubister soon after winning the award, including the PS: 'Could you please forward a copy of this letter to Mr Dennis, as I don't have his address.')

Indulgent smiles were everywhere to be seen on the Coulthard table, none bigger than that on the face of David Leslie. 'It was an absolutely fantastic night. My father and I both felt so proud to have been able to help David to get to that stage in his career. I'd won the Grovewood Award some years earlier, which was a similar sort of thing, so it was very pleasing to see a driver I was involved with winning the new equivalent. We definitely felt right then that David was on the path to the very top.'

They were not alone. Among those present that night was Jackie, now Sir Jackie, Stewart. Two years earlier JYS had set up a racing team to help further his son Paul's motorsport ambitions. Paul ran the team, which took his name, as well as driving for PSR in Formula 3 and, later, in Formula 3000. For 1990 Paul and Jackie were on the lookout for a young driver on

the up, to help promote and develop the team's 'Staircase of Talent' programme. Its philosophy was simple. The chosen prodigy would join PSR at the team's first level, the new Formula Vauxhall Lotus category. If successful he would progress to Formula 3 and then to Formula 3000. If all went perfectly the driver would graduate to F1 with barely a ruffled feather. Guidance, counsel, even coaching, would all be taken care of under the eye of a grand prix great.

David's position as one of Britain's most talented and promotable young racers made him eminently suitable for PSR's ambitions. He was also Scottish, as were most of those around him. Between the Coulthards, the Leslies, the Stewarts, and the Foubisters, David's early career had a distinctly north-of-the-border flavour.

Paul Stewart, who moved quickly to begin discussions with David Leslie as to Coulthard's plans, admits the clans were working with rare harmony. 'We had followed what DC had been doing, and because of what you might call the Scottish mafia there was a natural interest. We spoke with David Leslie and ended up offering DC a drive. Our first impressions were of a very professional young guy. We had to keep him off the car, he was so keen. He wanted to help out but we had to explain that the mechanics would be taking care

Jackie and Paul Stewart had great ambitions for Paul Stewart Racing and their 'staircase of talent' programme. They realised their dreams when Stewart Grand Prix became an F1 team in 1997.

The reward for winning the McLaren/ *Autosport* Young Driver of the Year award was a test-drive in a McLaren F1 car. The picture betrays David's nervous excitement as he prepares to experience the power of a Formula 1 car. It wouldn't be the last time...

of that now. Like all drivers he had a certain high level of determination and you could certainly sense that from him. That and his talent.'

David's team-mate that year would be the Brazilian Gil de Ferran and the pair quickly became friends. They still holiday together and David is godfather to Gil's daughter. 'They had a good chemistry almost immediately,' says Stewart, 'in fact the team as a whole was a good place to work that year. They were competitive as team-mates but everything was done in a good spirit.' Their friendship owed much to being thrown together off-track as well as on. David and Gil both rented accommodation near PSR's base at Milton Keynes, 50 miles (80km) north of London, to be closer to the team. Gil remembers they were two young guys a long way from home with very little to do. 'We were thrust into life in Milton Keynes – ha! Not that there's anything particularly bad about Milton Keynes, but neither DC nor I had any friends or family there. It was pretty much him and me. Clearly there was no support system, so we used to spend all

day every day at the factory. We spent an awful lot of time together.'

The proximity might have brought enmity had it not been for Gil's finding David's peccadilloes endearing. 'Man, he was *so* clean! He must be the cleanest guy I ever knew, honestly. He used to come to my flat for dinner and it was, man, terribly messy. He used to clear up for me – it was the first thing he would do even before he had sat down. He was unbelievable! Once he had done that he wouldn't mind me starting to cook. I used to tell him he had ruined the character of my flat! I guess he's just a clean sort of dude.'

They raced together all year for the series' European and British titles, sharing cars and hotels at each event. 'We used to drive to all of the races together, all over Europe, and it was always pretty cool, actually. He's not a mysterious sort of guy. He's pretty straightforward and I guess we were able to keep the competitive spirits at the race tracks.' Most of the time. Zolder that year, the second round of the Euroseries, provided a brief flashpoint for the two amigos.

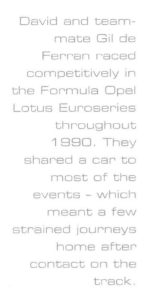

David and team-mate Gil de Ferran raced competitively in the Formula Opel Lotus Euroseries throughout 1990. They shared a car to most of the events – which meant a few strained journeys home after contact on the track.

'Yeah,' smiles Gil, 'it wasn't so great. We had qualified mid-grid; we certainly weren't one-two, but at the end of the first lap he dived straight into the chicane and flattened my right rear tyre. I couldn't believe he had hit me, the bastard! My tyre was done and that was it. I don't think Jackie was too happy.' And they had to drive home together from Belgium to Milton Keynes... 'The beginning was a little bit tense, but by half distance it was like "Yeah, whatever". At least it proved our friendship was strong enough to survive a test.'

David had been a strong favourite to continue the unbroken run of success that had lasted since '83, but the challenge of Vauxhall Lotus proved tougher than expected. He ended the season in only fourth place in the British championship and fifth in its European counterpart. He did not win a race until round four, at Silverstone, and the season also brought his first serious motorsport injury.

Round eight of the European series was held at the Spa-Francorchamps circuit, in Belgium. At the end of

the first lap, David's car, running fifth, was nudged into a spin, and then gently into the barriers, by Swedish driver Kenny Brack. David had kept the engine running, but his car was facing the wrong way. As he attempted to restart with a half-spin, a fast-approaching Alain Plasch spotted Coulthard, became distracted, and also spun – straight into David's car. The impact between the rear of Plasch's car and the nose of David's was heavy and unpleasant to witness. 'I remember looking up and seeing Alain coming straight at me backwards,' said David. 'I couldn't move, I couldn't do anything. It's that sort of time you wish you were somewhere else.'[1]

Both drivers needed medical attention at the scene. Plasch was concussed and spent the night in hospital; David was limping but thought nothing more of it. Back in the pits, however, there was drama. Spa is a long circuit, running through woodland, and once David left the car the team lost contact with him. 'It was traumatic for us,' says Paul Stewart. 'All we knew was that there had been an accident and we had lost our driver. No one knew where he was or where he had gone off.

David had just vanished. It filtered back as a potential horror story. It's really quite a distressing thing for a team when something like this happens, particularly because we had David's family there with us.' Jackie Stewart went to work and found that David had been flown to a hospital outside the circuit. Drama over. The calmest PSR employee during those tense moments had been their injured driver. When he later returned to the pits he couldn't work out what all the fuss was about.

He might not have been so calm had he known that his right lower leg had been broken. The fracture was not diagnosed until David returned home and it was serious enough to keep him out of the cockpit for a month. It scuppered his chances of fighting for either Vauxhall Lotus title. If he was frustrated, he didn't let it show. 'There was never any drama or complaint from DC,' says Paul Stewart, 'that's just the way he is. It's not that he's not an emotional individual – quite the contrary. It just wasn't something that I ever heard him moan about.'

Remarkably, David even tried to help another driver, Scott Lakin, during his enforced absence. Scott's manager at the time was Jim Wright, now commercial director of BMW.WilliamsF1. Wright approached Paul Stewart about Scott taking Coulthard's place while his leg healed, and was surprised to find David encouraging the move. 'That's pretty unheard-of behaviour for a racing driver,' says Wright, 'but he and Scott were quite good friends. In the event it didn't happen, for financial reasons, but at least DC tried. It would have been easier for him to do the opposite.'

The injury gave David a period in which to reflect, for the first time since '83. While he would not have believed it then, the enforced lay-off was almost certainly beneficial. Jackie Stewart remembers David at that time as 'a young driver of great talent', but one who 'struggled at first with the mind management side of things'. 'How to control your head in difficult circumstances is one of the most challenging issues for a racing driver,' he continues. 'Gil de Ferran learned how to do it, as we saw in 2003 when he won at Indianapolis while he was still recovering from serious back injuries. But it doesn't happen overnight. A competitor in any sport has to know how to regroup

and re-focus. Gil dealt with it then; I've seen David do it as he matured. It's the one thing that's shared by all the really good drivers and David had to learn it.'

Stewart's critical gaze identified other areas of the Coulthard package in need of fine-tuning. He suffered – still suffers – from what Stewart describes as an inability to alter his driving style to compensate for inadequacies in a car's performance or handling. While David's scent for perfection made him a formidable rival when he was able to tune the car to his precise needs, mechanical inadequacies would hamper him more than they would some other drivers. Dave Boyce had noticed this when he ran David in karts; other race engineers would echo the sentiment when he reached Formula 1. 'David struggled with that quite a lot at first,' says Stewart. 'He would be unhappy if there was a technical weakness, it would unsettle him. He has always had great driving skills, great car control. But when the car was not 100 per cent, it became difficult for him. It was not in his repertoire to compensate for his car's inadequacies or imbalance by altering his driving technique.'

For the first time, David was learning what it meant to work in an environment where even the most minute weaknesses were scrutinised and where failure to improve was simply not an option. It was demanding, but the training David received at PSR had been invaluable preparation for the questions that were asked of him when he made his dramatic Formula 1 debut.

[1] *Autosport*, 30 August 1990.

That familiar thousand-yard stare as David prepares for battle. The cockpit of a Formula 1 car is the only place where he feels truly alone, he says.

fixing
a hole

David Coulthard's last race for Williams had ended with a whimper and a bang, his car skewed into the pit wall of the Adelaide circuit. It was a harmless accident, no damage done to anything other than David's pride and a few FW17 suspension parts.

Earlier that weekend his McLaren team-mate-to-be, Mika Häkkinen, had suffered an accident of an altogether more violent nature. In Friday afternoon practice, as he entered the fast, fourth-gear right-hander that exited onto the back straight, Dequetteville Terrace, the left rear tyre of his McLaren deflated suddenly. It was later found to have a four-inch cut in the rubber, most likely to have been picked up from debris on the track. The red-and-white car slewed to the left, and Häkkinen lost control at more than 130mph (210kph). The car was travelling almost backwards as it hit kerbing at the edge of the track and took off, launching into a low flight towards a single-layer tyre barrier. The impact was stark, the deceleration savage. Mika's car thudded in at around 125mph (200kph) and his helmet hit the car's steering wheel. Once again images of a driver slumped motionless in the cockpit, head flopped to the left, were being broadcast from a Formula 1 event. 1994 and '95 were dangerous years.

The emergency medical team led by Dr Jerome Cockings of the Royal Adelaide Hospital arrived swiftly. Their actions saved Häkkinen's life. An emergency resuscitation procedure known as a cricothyroidotomy was performed at the track and minutes later Mika's limp body was unfolded onto a stretcher. Cockings

later paid tribute to Professor Sid Watkins, the Formula 1 medical delegate, who, he said, had played a vital role in ensuring the operation was smoothly effected. Their actions in restoring Häkkinen's oxygen supply prevented his suffering any brain damage. It is extremely rare for any head injury victim not to suffer simultaneous brain injury. Mika Häkkinen was one of the exceptions.

Disturbing photographs show Mika being lifted from the cockpit, helmet off, clotted blood across his nose, lips and mouth, eyes open but lifeless. He looked like a puppet without strings. Beneath his familiar floppy blonde fringe, Mika's skull had been cracked by the impact. Within half an hour he was on a respirator in the intensive care ward of the Royal Adelaide Hospital. It seemed impossible that just a day later McLaren principal Ron Dennis was telling journalists Mika had regained consciousness and was asking questions about what had happened. Mika had said he remembered a pain in his throat as the resuscitation procedure was performed. He said he remembered coming round and seeing Sid Watkins, Ron Dennis, and Ron's wife, Lisa, who was holding Mika's hand.

The talk was of a 'swift return' to the cockpit and a full season ahead at McLaren. But those who had seen this sort of thing before were sceptical. Aside from the physical wounds, the mental scars of a head injury might never heal. Eighteen months earlier Sauber driver Karl Wendlinger had been in a coma after his head received a heavy blow in an accident at the Monaco Grand Prix. He had since returned to Formula 1, but he

had lost his speed and complained of terrible headaches whenever he drove for a prolonged period. Few believed Häkkinen would be any less afflicted, if, indeed, he was ever fit to return.

Häkkinen's accident was to colour his whole working life with Ron Dennis. After two difficult seasons, '94 and '95, during which Mika's commitment to the McLaren cause never wavered, Ron, at some level, felt that he owed Mika, who was then still to win a grand prix. Now that Mika had almost died in one of his cars, the debt had grown. Frank Williams spoke of a similar feeling of responsibility and of the 'simply immense sadness' shortly after Ayrton Senna's death – but he never had the opportunity to make amends. As Häkkinen eased back into the light, Dennis, at his bedside, resolved to do all he could to repay his driver.

Some years later, he admitted the accident had been responsible for forming a special bond between him and Häkkinen. 'There is a perception that I have a closer relationship with Mika than with David,' he said. 'There is the emotional value in that, but you've got to understand where it comes from. Walking into that Adelaide hospital I got sucked into the trauma of the whole thing. I got involved mentally in the milestones of Mika's recovery up until the point where he was up and running again. You're not human if that doesn't affect you, but it doesn't mean diddly-squat when I have to take decisions about the outcome of a grand prix and who's going to win. This doesn't mean I favour Häkkinen over Coulthard at all. We are a team who are focused on winning and that is what matters. Both drivers have our full and equal backing.'[1]

The accident and its effect on Dennis's relationship with Häkkinen would also come to colour David's relationship with his boss, although not at first. Indeed, when David arrived at McLaren, the overriding feeling throughout his new team was one of relief. 'At last we have the perfect line-up to fit our philosophy of building up a strong team with young drivers,' said Norbert Haug, Mercedes's motorsport head.

David's was the face of the future – bright, optimistic, and without baggage. With these two drivers in harness McLaren could at last look forward to a period of stability, their driver line-up having been unsettled since Senna left at the end of '93. Häkkinen had been a constant, but the second seat had been

occupied by Martin Brundle, Phillipe Alliot, Jan Magnussen, Mark Blundell… and Nigel Mansell.

Mansell's brief tenure at McLaren represented the most extended spell of public humiliation the team had ever endured. Dennis once remarked: 'I don't understand Nigel Mansell and I would never employ a driver I don't understand.' Yet for a period in '95, Dennis did just that. Their five months together did nothing to abate the sense of mutual incomprehension. Jo Ramirez, then McLaren's team co-ordinator, recalls the period with a mixture of horror and time-distanced amusement. 'Even a year later Ron was still very, very sensitive about the whole Mansell affair. Everyone had been pushing so hard to get Nigel but Ron had massive doubts. He was really reluctant; he didn't think Nigel was the answer, but we did need a star driver. We had tried Brundle, we had tried Phillipe Alliot, but the sponsors were pushing for a bigger name.

'Nigel had become available after Williams decided they would keep David for '95. On paper, you know, it seemed to make sense. He had won the last race of '94 and lots of races before that. He had been World Champion in '92, he had won the Indycar title… I advised Ron to take the risk. But Ron didn't want to. In the end he was forced by the sponsors to get Nigel,

against his judgement – and he was proved right. Working with Nigel was the worst experience I ever had. He was unbelievable. He was just so strange – I never knew what the deal was. He was on a totally different wavelength to everyone else. If he was up, you had to be up. If he was down, you had to be down. I never really hit it off with him. I last saw him at Spa in 2002 and I walked a long way around the paddock to avoid him. '95 was a terrible year; the whole thing was a really bad experience.'

Mansell wasn't the only problem. The '95 McLaren chassis, MP4/10, was one of the worst the team had ever produced; the Mercedes engine, while powerful, was not the equal of the Renault or Ferrari motors. Mansell had expected a glorious season to put cherries on the icing. He lacked the motivation to sort a dog of a car. In his last race, the Spanish Grand Prix, he retired from 14th place, describing the car as 'undriveable', even as Mika Häkkinen battled on in fourth place.

'The next race was Monaco,' Ramirez remembers, 'and the weekend before, Ron and Martin [Whitmarsh, McLaren managing director] went down to see Nigel to have a very straight talk. It was agreed that Nigel wouldn't be racing any more for McLaren that year but McLaren still had to pay him off. That angered me. I still think Nigel was cynical about the whole thing. He

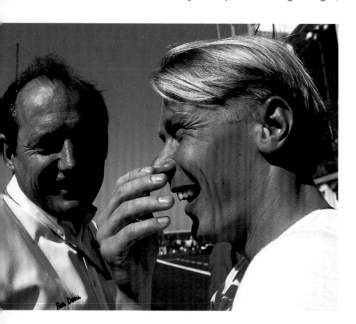

Ron Dennis and Häkkinen always enjoyed a close relationship. Dennis acknowledged this, but said the bond forged in the wake of Mika's accident never affected his judgement in any way that would harm the team.

Qualifying for the 1996 Australian Grand Prix was a wake-up call for David. He had never been so far back on an F1 grid. Helping to turn around a struggling team was a tougher challenge than running at the front in the best car on the grid.

knew how much he was worth at that moment and decided to take the money, even though he knew he didn't have it in him any more to be a Formula 1 driver. There are no half-measures in F1, but Nigel was nothing like at 100 per cent; even from the moment he signed he wasn't committed.'

After Mansell's last, inglorious Formula 1 race, Mark Blundell filled his vacated seat for the rest of the year. He impressed – but not enough, in Dennis's eyes, to make him change his mind about his '96 line up: Häkkinen and Coulthard.

Dennis had always believed in continuity and in nurturing talent from a young age; in Coulthard he had found an ideal protégé. A source close to Dennis recalls: 'I think Ron felt vindicated, to some extent, when he signed David. He had been the man he wanted for a couple of years and now he had him. He's very much like that as a boss. He will do what he has to do to get the person he wants, and even if he can't get them straight away, he'll wait until the time is right to make his move.'

After the Mansell debacle Ron kept his approaches to David very much to himself. This time, he insisted, things would be done his way. Says Jo Ramirez: 'The final decision over drivers is always Ron's of course, but with David, he was involved at every stage, even from the initial conversations with his manager Tim Wright. David had finished the season strongly for Williams and he was very much a character who would fit in well with the team. He was probably what we needed at the time. A Jacques Villeneuve always speaks his mind and maybe he would not have been right as a McLaren driver – he and Ron would never get it together. Not that McLaren likes "yes" people, but they are more aware than other teams how difficult it is to get the money. You have hundreds of millions of dollars of

Häkkinen's return to the cockpit post-Adelaide 1995 was at the wheel of the ungainly MP4/10. He silenced any doubters by setting super-competitive lap-times wherever he drove.

Leading the San Marino GP for 19 laps helped increase David's standing within the team, but a win would prove elusive: the 1996 McLaren wasn't one of the team's best efforts.

sponsorship riding with your team and you like to have a driver who repays that in the right way. In that respect DC really fitted the bill.'

David would soon prove, with his determined race performances and with his ceaseless commitment to the team's off-track activities, that he scored in every area valued by McLaren. In addition to being a highly promising driver, he was an ideal employee – a loyal company man. David's motivation was two-pronged: as well as wanting to impress his new paymasters there was the added incentive of showing Williams they should have fought harder to keep him.

There was another, less talked-about factor. In a revealing interview some years later with *F1 Racing* magazine, David admitted that when he signed for McLaren, he had put financial considerations first: 'I believe that I was encouraged [by IMG] to move from Williams to McLaren earlier than would otherwise have

been the case, because of money. At that time I was very happy with the salary I had with Williams. It wasn't a lot, but I was very happy to be there. If you look at my performances in the second half of '95, I scored more points than Damon [David scored 36 points to Damon's 34 over the last ten rounds of the 17-round championship], so it was logical that I might be kept beyond the end of that year. But because of a big-money offer from McLaren I went from sitting on the front row of the grid in Adelaide in '95 to sitting 13th on the grid in Melbourne the following March. Suddenly the penny dropped that it had been a mistake to go for the money when I should have gone for performance. That's why I'll never make a move for money over performance again.'[2]

David was about to learn the hard way that speed is the only currency that truly matters in Formula 1: '96 was going to be a difficult year.

At first it didn't seem so bad. McLaren had lured back their '80s superstar, Alain Prost – winner of the '85, '86, and '89 World Championships with the team – to act as a 'consultant'. 'Bloody quick consultant,' one paddock wag remarked. Prost's role was to help test and develop the car, by providing a benchmark against which McLaren and Mercedes engineers could compare information coming from the less experienced race drivers. And if Prost's pace – none of which seemed to have been lost in the three years since he stopped racing – helped keep David and Mika on their toes, all well and good.

'The best testers drive at 95 per cent and use the other five per cent to think about the car and give feedback for the engineers,' Prost said. 'If I put pressure on David and Mika while I'm doing it, that's just part of the game. It's healthy competition.' Besides, he still loved driving racing cars: 'With this job it's like going out for dinner with a nice woman and not actually doing anything. It's still better than spending time with an ugly woman!'[3]

David's first run with his new team, at Jerez, was in December '95, almost exactly five years since he had first tested one of their cars as McLaren/*Autosport* Young Driver of the Year. Häkkinen was absent, of course, although McLaren were optimistic he would be able to test within the next month. In pictures at the time, however, Mika looked wasted and pale, fuelling speculation that David would be leading the team in '96 alongside Jan Magnussen, McLaren's test driver. Coulthard declined to comment on the rumours,

A chat with Adrian Newey on the grid at the Belgian Grand Prix. It wouldn't be long before David and Adrian renewed the partnership which had begun to flourish in 1995 at Williams.

preferring to concentrate on the task ahead. From the inside, he said, the MP4/10 which finished the '95 season didn't feel anything like as ungainly as it looked. But it *was* galling to see the Williams he had vacated lapping a second faster than he could manage at the same circuit. 'We're achieving 75 per cent of our potential,' he said. 'If the season were starting next week, I don't think we would be competitive.'

Not since '93, with Senna, had McLaren won a race. Their chances of doing so this year did not look good. But a new car brings renewed optimism and within weeks, McLaren's new MP4/11 was unveiled. The talk was of wins, better times ahead, high expectations.

The new car, which ran for the first time in February, looked much more of a racing machine than had its awkward, ugly predecessor. It had clean lines, and the hideous mid-wing mounted on the engine cover of the MP4/10 was gone. Alain Prost drove it first and was pleasantly surprised: 'The car responds well to changes and that is normally the sign of a good chassis.' Mercedes, starting the second year of their partnership with McLaren, had also improved their performance. The engine was now more 'driveable' thanks to smoother power delivery and a more even response to the throttle.

It seemed odd, though, that neither Häkkinen nor Coulthard, both of whom were at the Estoril test, had a run in the car. The start of the season was only three weeks away, on 10 March. Mika's absence from the cockpit was the more understandable as he was still regaining fitness, but David's had to be explained away in a few paragraphs of McLaren corporate 'spin'. 'The objective of any Grand Prix team,' said Ron Dennis, 'is to put both of its drivers in the best possible position to win races. If you have someone as knowledgeable and experienced as Alain, it would not be particularly clever not to draw on that experience. And you want it from the first person in the car. Both Mika and David understand that, even though they are itching to get driving.'[4]

This seemed fair enough, but a cynical press corps, gathered to witness the unveiling of the sleek new machine, could only interpret the words as a lack of complete confidence in the young 'uns. David remained

stoic: 'I think it's extremely positive that Alain's driving the car. He's there to be used as much as a driver wants. I want to learn as much as possible from him.'[5]

One of David's most remarkable qualities is his loyalty – particularly in adversity – but perhaps, on a day like this, a little outspoken pushiness would have been welcome, even if it had made things uncomfortable. But Gil de Ferran, David's close friend from junior racing days, believes that would be to misunderstand the Coulthard mentality: 'He's got a level head, you know he's not going to throw a wobbly or say stupid things that are destructive to the team spirit. As casual as he sometimes seems on the outside I know that inside him there's a guy who is super-committed and super-professional and tries extremely hard to do well. I know sometimes that does not come across, because he's so polite and he has been well brought up, but I know that inside the guy, there's true metal there. He's very determined and focused and he's just "all there" and that doesn't always come across, because he's so polite and unassuming and he doesn't like to talk about how good he is or can be.'

The measure of how good David would need to be in '96 would come, after all, from Mika Häkkinen. There was much interest in McLaren's new car that day at Estoril, but its launch was overshadowed by the return to public life of Mika, for the first time since his accident at Adelaide. Interest was stoked by the confirmation that he would race from the start of the season.

The team had been impressed by Häkkinen's strong testing form in the '95 car a week earlier at the Paul Ricard circuit in France. His lap times proved, to McLaren's relief, that while he had lost strength, he had lost none of his ability. Two weeks later (a week after Prost's first test of the new car) Mika took a turn at the wheel and set about showing the world – and David – that his speed remained intact. The McLaren was unable to match the pace of the Williams or Jordan cars, but Mika had a slight edge on his new team-mate. It was impressive from a man whose left eye was still 'lazy' and whose sense of balance had only been restored after doctors had operated on tiny bones within his ears. More than he might privately

Every now and again David got the chance to look down on his nemesis, Michael Schumacher. David and Michael would go wheel-to-wheel many times in their F1 careers.

have expected, after Häkkinen's dreadful accident, David had a fight on his hands.

The season started with Mika eight places ahead of him on the grid. When it ended, the qualifying tally read 12–4 in Mika's favour, and his eventual 31 points placed him fifth in the World Championship, to David's seventh on 18. Häkkinen's season had not been one of a man diminished. Still, David took the team's best finish of the year – second at a freaky Monaco – and he led for 19 laps at Imola before retiring. He also headed the field briefly at Spa, but the year's haul was poor. Over 16 races, his record read: retired, spun, 7th, 3rd, retired, 2nd, crashed, 4th, 6th, 5th, 5th, retired, spun, crashed, 13th, 8th. Not once did he get onto the front row of the grid; only twice did he get onto the second. At least there was the compensation of being worshipped by the team for his smooth ability with sponsors, media, and corporate guests.

Perhaps he was too smooth. Partnered with Häkkinen, David often found himself lumped with the lion's share of McLaren's PR duties. So unruffled was, and is, his manner, so polished his delivery in front of an audience, it has become received wisdom that David is 'good at PR'. This faintly damning praise carries with it the unspoken suggestion that being amenable to press and sponsors probably means he's too nice ever to achieve greatness. It is also indicative of subtle psychological pressure exerted upon him by Häkkinen. Friends and confidantes of Mika will tell how his sometimes monosyllabic manner was a carefully contrived artifice: let David be good at PR; I'll get on with the racing.

One McLaren employee, who was able to watch closely for several years how the two men tended their relationships with the press, has no doubt Häkkinen found an advantage through silence. 'David was always the good guy at press functions and it sometimes pissed him off that Mika was always so uncommunicative. There was a very subtle psychological thing going on there. It was part of Mika's armoury. He didn't let anybody come too close to him. Mika was afraid that if anyone got inside his head it could mess him up a bit. Between Didier Coton [Mika's manager], Mark Arnall [Mika's trainer] and Erja [Mika's wife] he had three very good lieutenants who kept everybody away from him. Occasionally at events Mika would get absolutely trollied on vodka and people would see that there's a completely different side to him, but at any other time he didn't let on. It was a very clever strategy.

'A great disappointment of mine is that Mika had this very strong support team around him, and without being derogatory in any way I think that DC has surrounded himself with mates who he is close to and who he knows and I think they are not necessarily what he needs. They have fun together, but perhaps they are not as clever at protecting him and helping him focus on the job in hand.'

That job, in '96, had proved particularly difficult, as David struggled to come to terms with a car little better than its maligned predecessor. The challenge from his team-mate had also been stronger than he had ever expected. Little did he know it then, but it was a battle that would go on for another five seasons, as his partnership with Häkkinen became the longest-running driver pairing F1 had known.

How right he had been when he noted, on the eve of his first season with the team that would become his racing 'home': 'Ron has said before that he wants to see drivers start and end their careers at McLaren. Sometimes things occur which means that doesn't happen, but I certainly plan to be here for quite a long time. I think I get on well enough with Ron for that to happen.'[6]

[1] *Autosport*, 17 May 2001.

[2] *F1 Racing*, November 2002.

[3] *F1 Racing*, April 1996.

[4] *Autosport*, 15 February 1996.

[5] Ibid.

[6] *Autosport*, 14 December 1995.

One highlight of David's 1993 season was winning his class at Le Mans in a Tom Walkinshaw-prepared Jaguar XJ220. David has said he would like to race again at Le Mans, 'with a few friends, for fun'.

money – that's what i want

The British Formula 3 title is one of motorsport's glittering prizes. Any young driver with ambition wants it tattooed onto his CV. In 1991, with a patchy season of Formula Vauxhall Lotus behind him, David Coulthard wanted it more than most. He ran through the list of Formula 1 champions and race winners who had excelled in Formula 3, imagining his name alongside theirs: Emerson Fittipaldi, Nigel Mansell, Nelson Piquet, Ayrton Senna, Jody Scheckter, Jackie Stewart…

Stewart, in fact, would be David's boss again that season, at Paul Stewart Racing. Jackie and son Paul were aware of the lustre of the British F3 title and it was one of their greatest ambitions that Paul Stewart Racing should claim the prize. Paul himself had raced in Formula 3 in '89 and '90 without ever having been a title contender. In '91 David would lead the PSR challenge.[1]

His Ralt RT35 chassis looked very 'team Scotland' as it was wheeled out of PSR's workshop. The Scottish driver and team owners the world already knew about; they had Scots backing to match: Highland Spring; Tunnock's biscuits; Kwik-Fit (owned by Scot Tom Farmer), and, still prominent, Hayton Coulthard. Numerous indeed are the corporate vaults cracked open by a JY Stewart charm offensive; he is not a man easily denied. 'Aye,' says Sir Jackie, eyes a-twinkle, 'I just went out and sold PSR.'

In the 1991 British F3 season, the Paul Stewart Racing-Coulthard combination was often the one to beat. David won more races than any other driver, but Rubens Barrichello took the title.

Finished in patriotic blue and white, and complemented by David's saltire helmet, the car looked fabulous. It was unfortunate for the team that rivals were as inclined to look daggers in their direction as they were to gaze in envy. Many F3 veterans resented PSR's presence. The more cynical regarded the team as little more than a rich man's folly, despite the presence on their staff of quality personnel such as Andy Miller, David's race engineer. It was a notion Paul Stewart was itching to disabuse. Undeniably PSR had been founded by Sir Jackie for Paul to run; undeniably PSR went about their business very seriously – and with an edge of ruthlessness.

The team had grown close to David and Gil de Ferran during their year together in Formula Vauxhall Lotus in '90; both were highly rated. But when the time came to finalise the drivers for the '91 F3 campaign, Gil was out. He was replaced for part of the season by Eduar Mehry Neto, then by Andre Ribeiro from round 11 onward, as the team sought to balance the books. 'We had to make some tough choices and one of them was to let Gil go,' Paul Stewart reflects. 'That was hard, although he did come back to us. Without Gil all our hopes rested with David that year.'

He faced challenges from Rubens Barrichello, Rubens's team-mate at West Surrey Racing, Jordi Gene, and from Rickard Rydell in the TOMs Toyota. All were aggressive, talented young drivers, each racing to prove the future was theirs. Rydell and Barrichello won the first two rounds, as David struggled to find the speed in qualifying which would take him to the tip of the sharp end.

This weakness was mystifying for a driver otherwise so complete, but it was a blind spot which would blight his career. David was always capable of the single, irresistible pole position lap, as he would prove a decade later at the 2001 Monaco Grand Prix. Yet he was equally capable of indifferent qualifying sessions

Throughout a close-fought season, David battled with other leading runners Rubens Barrichello, Rickard Rydell, and Hideki Noda. Here he chases Rydell on the opening lap at Donington.

whenever his confidence was rattled by a less-than-perfect car. He learned to compensate with another talent: 'He is simply one of the best starters in the history of the sport,' reckons Jackie Stewart.

As the teams arrived at the Thruxton circuit for round three, his start-line magic had yet to work. He needed a win to inject life into his title challenge, but qualifying remained a problem. David lined up fourth for the race – not bad in itself, but behind his three major rivals, each of whom could be expected to mount a robust defence of their position.

Race start. Coulthard immediately into second from fourth. Half a lap later he was through into the lead. It remained his to the flag. This became a consistent theme: what David lacked in qualifying he could make up in a few seconds of explosive aggression at the start of the race. Paul Stewart had a ringside view all year and he still smiles at the memory: 'Normally in F3, if you didn't qualify well you'd be stuffed. But David didn't seem to have heard that one. At the time I had never seen a driver be able to win from where he could come from. To this day I don't think I've seen another do it quite as well.'

It helped that Rubens Barrichello, David's principal opponent, had terrible trouble getting off the line, despite being the season's unofficial qualifying 'king', with nine pole positions. 'Yeah, we never used to worry about Rubens being on pole, which he often was,' says Stewart. 'David had such confidence at the start and such a relish for wheel-to-wheel stuff that when the lights went green he would be up to second or third from the third or fourth row and then challenging for the lead a lap or two later. It's just something DC does. I don't think he has to focus particularly hard or think about it too much to get a good start. He's quite nonchalant about it.'

The confidence he showed in powering through had an important psychological effect on his rivals. In much the same way that Stirling Moss in his heyday would make sure he looked extra-cocky and relaxed in the hour before a wet race – the better to destabilise opponents fearful of damp conditions – David would look chipper and eager as he settled into a car which would start from the upper midfield. Like a self-fulfilling prophecy, he would make a good start because the drivers around him *knew* he was going to make a good start. At Silverstone in June he won from

seventh, in wet conditions. This type of performance was very much against the natural order of things in Formula 3 and David's rare blend of abilities had started to come to the attention of Frank Williams. His performance at Silverstone led directly to the later offer of a Williams test drive.

David won three more times that season, to take his total for the season to five, and went to the last round, at Thruxton, needing one more victory to take the title, provided Barrichello finished fourth or lower. David qualified seventh, Rubens on pole, but given their respective starting records that season, a win for David still seemed possible. He got up to third, attempted to pass Hideki Noda for second, but they crashed, ending David's race and championship ambitions.

It had been an impressive year, one which made up for the disappointment of the abortive '90 season in Formula Vauxhall Lotus. The title had slipped away, but David had proved himself an aggressive racer and a multiple winner (including victory mid-season at the prestigious Marlboro Masters of Formula 3 event, at the Zandvoort track in Holland). Most importantly, his career once again had direction. Formula 3000, the

established feeder category to Formula 1, was the obvious next step.

But David wasn't quite finished with Formula 3. There was the small matter of the Macau Grand Prix to attend to. This classic event, held around a circuit traced from the streets of the Portuguese protectorate which nestles in the shadow of mainland China, holds the kudos of a national Formula 3 title, all on its own. Winners here can boast of their victory as proudly as they can any number of domestic championship wins. In Formula 3 terms, Macau matters, and for David it presented the perfect opportunity to push aside the disappointment of not having won the British F3 title. The demands of the circuit corseted by concrete and steel are exceptional: it punishes the smallest mistake. Drivers arrive from around the world to race there, creating a field of unmatched quality. Ayrton Senna won in '83; seven years later Mika Häkkinen and Michael Schumacher contested a head-to-head so fierce it passed into motorsport legend. Macau is also lucrative. In '91 the winning driver would pocket around £30,000. For a skint F3 pedaller, that's serious cash.

But before the race, the partying. Among F3 team

A clash with Hideki Noda at the final round scuppered David's 1991 F3 title hopes. A bent front wing meant a visit to the pits, which put him out of contention. Many felt David was the year's moral champion.

David cleans his kit before the Macau GP – not surprising for a man known to towel down shower doors to get rid of the drips. Gil de Ferran reckons Coulthard is one of the tidiest men alive.

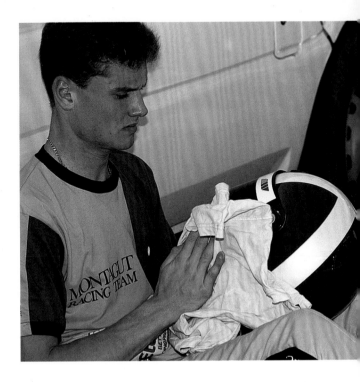

Dave Stubbs (far left), team manager at Paul Stewart Racing, had to intervene on occasion to keep the peace between Paul Stewart and Coulthard. Although Paul and David remain good friends, tempers ran high when they were team-mates.

PSR's cars always looked the part, even if their performance was hampered in 1992 by their Judd engines. David is in centre frame preparing to go out for practice at Enna, in Sicily.

personnel and journalists Macau was infamous for providing a mighty end-of-season bash, one in which the drivers, too, engaged with gusto. Stewart Williams, who covered the '91 Macau race for the weekly motor-racing newspaper *Motoring News*, recalls it fondly: 'Macau was fantastic. The circuit was crazy, with concrete and barriers everywhere and gradients so steep it was hard to walk up them. The best young drivers in the world were there and they were all free from the pressure of their championships. All they had to do was race and have a good time. Qualifying was always on the Friday and the race was on Sunday, so they didn't have much to do on the Saturday. Friday night was pretty much 'game on'. I remember being in some hotel nightclub or other, baling out in a pretty poor state at about 5am, and there were still drivers in there, pushing on until daylight. I think the best you can say for them is that they didn't drink the night before the race. At least, I don't think they did.'

David Coulthard was one of those who managed to practise abstinence. He had broken his qualifying hoodoo by putting in the second-fastest lap of the weekend and there was every chance he could leave Macau a winner.

The race was held over two heats; the overall winner would be the man who put in the best performances over both. DC made the best possible job of round one: he won after passing Rickard Rydell for the lead on lap two. Heat two wasn't too shabby, either: he built a ten-second lead but finished a close second after letting Jordi Gene through to the flag. *Motoring News*'s correspondent thought he had seen the performance of a young man who had just guaranteed his future. 'We had all been expecting a titanic battle between David and Jordi and it was fabulous to watch,' said Williams. 'They were trading fastest lap times in the race – times which were better than their qualifying laps, but in the end David had it under control. It was a bloody good performance.'

The Coulthard-PSR relationship was enjoying a belated honeymoon period. They hadn't won the championship together, but they had been within reach of it, and in getting so close had proved the team's credibility. With the momentum gained from

Macau, team and driver headed into the winter in good spirits. David was content that after an excellent season he could be confident of success in F3000. His boss, Paul, was equally optimistic. He would be driving alongside David in the team's second chassis, and anticipated a season of 'win-win' for himself and PSR. If David was successful, the team would be too; if Paul was successful, he would prove himself both as driver and as team principal.

It was a demanding challenge for Stewart, but not one that he feared: 'Whenever I was in a racing car I was a driver. There was no management stuff interfering. I was never fearful of having good drivers as my team-mates, because having good drivers was good for the team and for the company. I didn't want to put someone in just so that I could look good. I think, though, that DC found that a little unusual and maybe harder to deal with. Of course he wanted to beat me as his team-mate, but I don't think he could understand at first how I gained satisfaction from seeing another driver in the team do well even at times when I hadn't done so well.'

What no one had predicted was that both drivers were in for a torrid season: '92 was dreadful for PSR. Hampered by Judd engines which were not fully competitive until the end of the year, David and Paul could achieve only ninth and 13th places in the championship. There were times in '92 when the team's famous name seemed more burden than blessing.

A fractious pre-season test set the tone. David and Paul were lapping Spain's Jerez circuit together when the two of them almost crashed at high speed. David had been on a fast lap while Paul was cruising back to the pits. As David entered the double right-hander at the end of the lap, fully committed to his cornering line, Stewart crossed his path. The Coulthard red mist descended and he stormed back to the pits to confront Stewart over what he thought had been a crass, even dangerous, piece of driving. Boss or no boss, Paul was about to get a piece of his mind.

'Those two corners at the end of the lap, were bloody fast,' Stewart says. 'It was where Martin Donnelly had that dreadful accident in the Lotus in 1990. As I came in, DC was driving behind me. He came up to me in the middle and I moved to get out of his way. Unfortunately he thought I had tried to take him off. We got back to the pits and, yes, it got a bit heated between us. It ended up with Dave Stubbs, the team manager, almost physically hauling us out of the cars, dragging us round to the back of the team truck and giving us a massive dressing down. He'd seen it all before with young drivers and he wasn't about to have two of his taking each other off the track. He did give us quite a bollocking. It's amusing now, although at the

Keith Wiggins's Pacific team were known for squeezing good results from a tight budget. David managed to finish third in the 1993 championship with them, and he won the Enna round.

Pacific's Cosworth engines were far more competitive than the Judd motors DC had used at Paul Stewart Racing in 1992. David relished the extra power and reliability.

time it didn't seem so funny. Neither of us were laughing that particular day.'

Stewart considers the incident to have been a revealing flash of the hidden Coulthard temperament. 'He's a fantastic guy, really, truly – one of my very best friends. But he can lose it. DC at that time was quite set on showing everybody that he was the number one driver. I think that eventually it was understood. It didn't come between us, anyway.'

Unfortunately for the team, they needed more than David's hidden passion to bring success. 1992's vogue was for a Reynard 92D chassis coupled with a Cosworth engine. PSR had the right car, but their Judd motor was horsepower-shy. Down on power and short of luck, David started the season, at Silverstone in May, on the back row of the grid. He had spun off in rain during the qualifying session and could only watch from the sidelines as his boss put in a lap good enough for sixth on the grid. His performance had not been helped by a dispute with his management which was resolved only a short time before the practice session. David turned the tables in the race, sneaking through to a seventh place finish, one position ahead of Paul, but still his debut had been pointless in every sense. David, in fact, did not score until round seven at Spa-Francorchamps, where he finished fourth.

Laughter was in fairly short supply at PSR in '92,

although Paul does remember a degree of strained humour at wandering into the team truck one race morning, ready to change into his race suit and flameproof underwear, only to find 'someone' had cut the sleeves from the jersey he wore beneath his suit. The culprit? 'Oh I couldn't possibly comment. I'm convinced to this day that it was David, as part of his plan to out-psyche and intimidate me. At the time I thought it was below the belt, but I can just about laugh about it now.'

The season's last two races at Nogaro and Magny-Cours were better, bringing DC a pair of thirds, but when he looked back over the final standings he could not escape the fact that, for the first time in his career, he had driven a season without winning a race. For a driver with intentions to go all the way, this was bad news. Career plateaus are the enemy of a racing driver's ambition. A moment's hesitation and someone younger, more fashionable, is on your shoulder, then through, ahead, gone, to take the success and acclaim that had seemed within reach.

This was a tricky time for David. His relationship with PSR had been built on the expectation of mutual success, but with nothing better than a brace of thirds to boast about, the partnership looked unstable. The team wanted top dollar (roughly £400,000 to £500,000) to give David another season: nothing personal, that was just the way it worked. David,

acting on his father's counsel, decided to look elsewhere. His manager at the time, Tim Wright of IMG, advised them to contact Pacific Racing. The team, led by Keith Wiggins, had a reputation for achieving good results on tight budgets.

David brought little cash to the table other than backing from his father and one or two personal sponsors. After three seasons enjoying the relative splendour of Paul Stewart Racing, Pacific bore the taste of motor racing the way David had first got used to it: no money, no frills. Motorhome luxury was out. Wives and girlfriends of all team personnel – drivers included – were expected to help out on the domestic front. 'Most of them didn't mind,' recalls Mark Gallagher,

A brush with officialdom. Coulthard and team-mate Michael Bartels seem resigned to following orders at Spa in 1993. Bartels had been tipped for great things, but his career faded as David's prospered.

then Pacific's marketing and PR man, 'but I'm not sure how keen David's girlfriend, Andrea Murray, was. She was an absolute stunner, it has to be said, and she was modelling, so maybe our image wasn't quite right for her. I remember thinking that somehow it made sense for David to have a Formula 1 girlfriend even before he had got to Formula 1.'

Whatever money the team could muster had to go on the racing. Whistling through his teeth, Keith Wiggins confirms that stories of the team's penury were not exaggerated: 'We had one particularly savage engine blow-up at Donington. The engine was completely lunched. Took me a couple of years to pay that one off.' But despite the lack of funding there was a good 'vibe' about the team, and Wiggins had a good gut feeling about DC: 'He hadn't had a great year in '92, but it was still pretty clear at that stage that he was one of the talents in F3000. We knew money would be tight for the year but we thought there was enough to do OK. We were pretty sure DC was the guy for the job and there was definitely a mood of wanting to make something happen that year.'

But when? At the first race of the year, Donington, David looked to be in for another '92: 14th on the grid, blown engine in the race. Silverstone, one week later, was better. Qualifying was poor again – ninth – but on Sunday afternoon he put in one of the drives of his career to date. Fifth by lap two, he was up to third by lap 15, behind his old boss Paul Stewart and his old mucker Gil de Ferran, back with PSR.

Stewart remembers their squabble over second place (eventually won by David) as 'a right old ding-dong'. 'We had an almighty battle. I remember Gil winning because he had built up a bit of a lead, but David came through from a poor grid position and really started giving me a hard time. It was quite aggressive racing but I was never unfair with him and he was never unfair with me. He did pass me in the end, the bastard! I guess that's why he's in F1 and why I decided not to go any further than F3000.'

Stewart's tone is gently rueful, but his words are shot through with respect for David's fighting qualities. Gil de Ferran, who won that afternoon at Silverstone, is another who knows them well: 'As a driver? He's a bulldog! He's

certainly one of the best guys I ever raced against, especially in terms of the wheel-to-wheel stuff – to the point where he would make you frustrated at not being able to drop him. He knows how to place the car well in a fight. That's why he's so good at starts and when he's fighting for position and on first laps. That's his best quality, his highlight, if you like. All the really good guys have something that stands out and that's DC's. I remember several times when we were racing together and I qualified ahead of him. I'd think, "OK, there's no way I'm going to be seeing this guy again," but by the end of the first lap I'd be thinking, "Oh my God, he's right behind and he wants to come through." I remember an F3 race like that and it was like, "Fuck this".'

David battled again at Pau, round three, where he escaped a brush with the barriers to finish second. Then came Enna, the Sicilian sizzler. Here, for the first time in almost 18 months, David remembered what it took to win a motor race – despite the best efforts of Pedro Lamy. The pint-size Portuguese and David had clashed during the closing stages of race as Lamy barged his way into the lead. As they crossed the start/finish line on lap 36, Lamy raised a fist in a victory salute – but he had been given duff information by his pits: there was still a lap to go. To David's great amusement Lamy spun out 200 yards (180m) later.

Lamy's tough day was about to get tougher. As he trudged back to the paddock, he was caught up by David, who hadn't forgotten their incident. A friend of David's remembers the comedy of seeing a 5ft 10in (1.75m) Coulthard march down the paddock behind the 5ft 2in (1.55m) Lamy, prodding him in the back repeatedly, saying: 'don't – ever – do – that – to – me – again.'

His anger had subsided a little by the time of the podium ceremony, and as David stood on the top step in the swelter and dust, many thought they were looking at that year's F3000 champion. But it wasn't to be. The two German races at the Nürburgring and Hockenheim brought no points and there would be only one more podium finish – third – at Spa. The only other highlight for David that year came with a class win at Le Mans for the TWR team, driving a Jaguar XJ220.

David's mixed bag of strong results and abject retirements placed him third in the F3000 standings, but it was a frustrated DC who watched that year's top two, champion Olivier Panis and Pedro Lamy, waltz off to F1 as he was left to work out how he could finance a third F3000 season. Mark Gallagher believes only the team's lack of cash had prevented David from being a genuine title contender. 'The season was characterised by the fact that although David was often struggling in qualifying he would race brilliantly. He kept very, very good race pace. That's what we felt about him over the course of the season. He was certainly fast enough and he certainly deserved a break. We just lacked a bit of budget to do enough testing which would have helped him in qualifying. We just didn't have the money to test and develop. The fact that he struggled in qualifying wasn't down to DC, it was down to the team.'

Pacific's bare shelves meant much of the season was spent chasing sponsors. Their pursuit brought inevitable moments of comedy – most notably over the weekend of the Spa race in Belgium. 'I was staying with Keith in Liège that weekend,' says Gallagher, 'and we had dinner with DC one evening. We left and were walking back to the hotel with DC telling us enthusiastically about a potential sponsor who had flown into town that afternoon and would be coming to the track to meet us. Naturally we were looking forward to meeting him. It was important at the time. We needed more money and it would be good for DC, for the team, and so on.

'Anyway, we were strolling along, chatting, as you do – me, Keith, David, and I think David's old friend David Cawthorne was there too. There's quite a big red light district in Liège and we were skirting it as we walked home. We were walking past one of these houses of ill repute, the sort where the young ladies show their wares in the window and suddenly this chap comes stumbling out of the door with his shirt and jacket hanging all over the place. He'd obviously been spending his expense account that evening … He stumbled out of the doorway, swung round and who should it be but DC's new sponsor! He had never met Keith before. He was perspiring heavily and I remember him wiping his hand on his jacket and then holding it out for Keith, saying, "Oh, hello, we've never met."

'We were all totally creased up at this. But DC was incredible. He kept his composure and said,

A winner's trophy at last in F3000. David's victory at Enna, in Sicily, was his only F3000 victory in two seasons. He wanted it to be the springboard to F1, but at the end of the 1993 season he was resigned to a third year of F3000.

"Keith, Mark, I would like to introduce you to…" He was completely unfazed and managed to retain his good manners.'

David would need all his composure that winter, as he left Pacific with nowhere to go. His father had told him he would no longer be able to fund David's racing and other offers were thin on the ground. There were a few dark moments of the soul in those winter months. 'Like any young driver he used to wonder whether or not he was going to make it,' says one friend. 'He always gave off an aura of complete confidence, but it was impossible to know how things were going to work out. He was pretty hard up, too. All his money had gone into racing and he had no idea where the next cheque was coming from.'

Tim Wright, however, had worked hard to maintain David's profile with Formula 1 team bosses, writing to each of them every Monday morning after a race with details of David's performances. The only reply he can remember receiving was from Williams's technical director Patrick Head. 'It was perfectly civil,' says Wright, 'quite funny, actually. It said something like: "Dear Tim. Many thanks for your regular briefings on David's race results. I am, however, quite ecologically minded and I do not think any more damage should be done to the rain forests in order to send these letters to Williams".'

By this time, anyway, David's career was being watched with interest by all Williams's senior personnel. Throughout '93 he had been employed by them as a freelance test driver, giving him hope for a future with the team.

He could never have imagined how his introduction would arrive.

[1] Paul Stewart Racing did not in fact win the British F3 title until 1996, with Ralph Firman. Jackie Stewart keeps the trophy in his office, 'in pride of place'.

David's joy on the Melbourne podium was unbridled – as was that of his delighted boss, Ron Dennis. Williams had been expected to dominate the race, and the season, but McLaren had shown they were ready to make a fight of the title.

when i'm 64

One day an old, grey man called David Coulthard will sit back in a familiar chair, in a familiar room, and sip a whisky quietly as he reflects on a long, largely successful career as a Formula 1 driver. The noise and thunder will seem a lifetime ago but yesterday. He will pause to reflect on victories taken, opportunities missed…

He might dwell a little longer on 1997 than on other years. It brought two excellent wins; at least two more slipped away. It could have been the year in which he established supremacy at McLaren; in fact, it was the year in which Mika Häkkinen finally took his first F1 win, to launch himself into two seasons of near-invincibility. Highs, lows; joy, and tears: it was the Formula 1 season from Drama Scripts Inc: it would yield a dashing new champion with a famous name (Jacques Villeneuve); an arch-rival who resorted to dirty tactics in his quest for the title (Michael Schumacher); stirring performances from new talents (Giancarlo Fisichella); and rousing cameos from old hands (Damon Hill).

The 1997 McLaren MP4-12 helped the team regain some of the competitive form for which they were famed. The season turned out to be a thriller and David was in the thick of the action all year.

It also featured a secondary plot enacted by the McLaren-Mercedes boys, with David and Mika regularly thrusting themselves onto centre stage. Their strong performances were welcome – even if a little surprising, given the team's recent struggles. But there was a sense of rebirth about McLaren in '97. Everything about the team seemed right for a step back towards the big time. After three seasons and 49 races in the wilderness, they were ready to emerge and remind a world which might have forgotten what McLaren were all about.

Their new car, the MP4-12, was beautiful. It had a new Mercedes engine, rumoured to be the most powerful on the grid. There was a new title sponsor, West, to replace Marlboro, whose red and white colours had been synonymous with McLaren since '74. That meant a dazzling new silver and black colour scheme, in deference to Mercedes's heritage and West's corporate identity. The drivers were unchanged,

bringing some welcome stability along with their speed. Everything *looked* perfect.

All was not quite as it seemed, however. The switch from Marlboro to West was presented in time-honoured McLaren fashion as a natural progression of corporate identity. But behind the scenes, there had been months of acrimony between the team and Philip Morris, owners of the Marlboro brand. Sponsorship requirements for '97 were discussed throughout April '96, during which time the two parties failed to agree on how much should be paid for title branding of a pair of Formula 1 cars. Philip Morris, and in particular their armour-plated sponsorship head John Hogan, wanted a cheaper deal than the $30 million per season McLaren were demanding. That would be a fair reflection, he said, of the team's decline in performance since '93. McLaren were not prepared to budge.

Hogan, who was appointed sporting director of Jaguar Racing in 2003, recalls: 'What it came down to

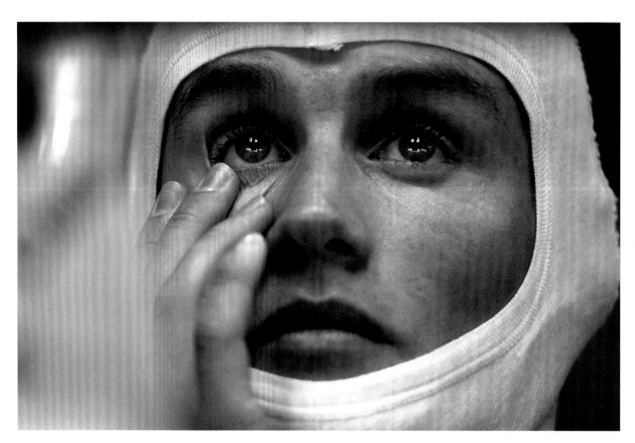

was this: McLaren had been three years without a win and they were still demanding top dollar. There comes a point where even in F1 big companies say, "Hang on, when we look at this from a return on the investment point of view, we are going to have to re-evaluate." We looked at what we were doing with McLaren and we looked at what we were doing with Ferrari and it became clear that we should be increasing our involvement with Ferrari. The decision was made in April '96. There are certain people at McLaren who maintain that they went after West and dumped Philip Morris. To that I can categorically say "Bollocks".'

Dennis at the time was somewhat more diplomatic: 'The change to West affords us the opportunity of implementing a more dynamic and exciting image that we believe is important for our future development and which is completely consistent with West's brand values. Philip Morris has been our staunchest supporter and contributor to our success over the years and we are disappointed that we were unable to reach an agreement.'

Whatever commercial anguish (and expediency) lay behind the shining new image, few could argue the new cars looked absolutely stunning. Grand prix aficionados recognised instantly the echo of Mercedes's 'Silver Arrows' machines from the '30s and '50s. Those were eras of great motorsport success for Mercedes and this deliberate harking back to the glory years seemed an unequivocal statement of intent. Likewise McLaren's widely-reported courting of Adrian Newey, the aerodynamics Svengali employed so gainfully at Williams as chief designer until the end of '96. He was tipped to be making a high-profile transfer to McLaren sometime in '97, having fallen out with his old team and been placed on so-called 'gardening leave'. Observers believed that were his talents to be added to the existing strengths of McLaren and Mercedes, the team could become untouchable. For now he

Eyes on the prize: David kept a clear focus on the challenge he faced from Mika Häkkinen. Mika was long overdue a grand prix victory and David knew that a first win could open the floodgates. . .

. . . there were some lighter moments that season however.

remained on Williams's payroll, awaiting resolution of his contractual dispute.

McLaren's driver pairing was one of the few areas of the team left alone. In pre-season testing their performances were close: at the last test session in Estoril before the MP4-12's official launch, David edged out Häkkinen. Their speed was encouraging, but after so many fallow years McLaren personnel were reluctant to make grand claims for the potential of the '97 package. Not that there was any modesty in the car's unveiling in late February. A grand affair at London's Alexandra Palace exhibition hall drew almost 5,000 journalists for the presentation of the new look. The Spice Girls, then in their Girl Power pomp, provided the tunes, along with Jamiroquai. After a

launch on this scale, any failure to deliver on the track would bring forth ridicule and contempt. Already there was dark talk from Germany that funding for the Mercedes F1 programme was only as solid as the results achieved. In '97 the partnership simply *had* to deliver.

When the teams gathered in Melbourne three weeks later, the tinsel of 'Ally Pally' had long been forgotten. The talk was of Williams and of how fast the new FW19 would be in the hands of Jacques Villeneuve and Heinz-Harald Frentzen. Damon Hill's plight in the lamentable Arrows drew the attention of the British tabloid press; Michael Schumacher's confidence that his new Ferrari could challenge the best gave a headline to the international media.

Out on his own at Melbourne, 1997: David had a clear run to the flag after Frentzen's retirement and Schumacher's late pitstop. The win had been unexpected and broke a long barren patch for McLaren.

Jo Ramirez, McLaren team co-ordinator, congratulates David after his famous victory. The team had not made any plans for a post-race party, but this was swiftly sorted.

Olivier Panis is carried into the emergency helicopter after his accident at the 1997 Canadian Grand Prix. David had dominated the race, but it was stopped after the accident – while he was in the pits – robbing him of a certain win.

McLaren... McLaren were left alone. They would figure in the race, of course, but after three years of disappointment little of substance was expected from the first weekend. Success, if it came, would arrive later in the year. Melbourne would be a Williams-Schumacher affair.

David Coulthard crossed the start/finish line on lap 58 of the '97 Australian Grand Prix to be greeted by the sight of Australia's three-time Formula 1 World Champion, Sir Jack Brabham, waving the chequered flag at him. David was crying. He had been crying for the whole of the last lap. He had known since the end of lap 57 that if he could keep his car on track he would take his first win for McLaren and the first win of the modern Formula 1 era for Mercedes. His tears watered a drought that had lasted for 49 races since Ayrton Senna's last win, with McLaren, at the '93 Australian Grand prix. 'I never thought I would cry,' David said afterwards, 'I didn't think I could be that emotional in a racing car, but it all just came out when I thought about what it would mean to everyone at McLaren and Mercedes. I had forgotten what it feels like to be a winner.'

The victory had been unexpected. David had even told Mercedes's motorsport chief Norbert Haug he would dye his hair silver should he win. (He was as good as his word, having his hair dyed two weeks later and at a stroke making himself look thirty years older.) This was more than a simple desire not to tempt fate. In qualifying, the pole position Williams-Renault of Jacques Villeneuve was more than two seconds a lap faster than David's McLaren, in fourth spot. It was obvious Jacques' lap had been something special, as he was a second-and-a-half faster than even his team-mate, Heinz-Harald Frentzen, who had qualified in second place in an identical car. Even so, the potential of the Williams was clear.

On performance alone this should have been Villeneuve's race. But at the start Jacques was slow away from the line, encouraging Eddie Irvine, starting from fifth in his Ferrari, to take a lunge at him into the first corner. They collided and both went out, along with Sauber's Johnny Herbert – the unfortunate victim of someone else's accident.

Frentzen led from Coulthard, the McLaren looking more of a threat to the Williams in the race than it had in qualifying. Michael Schumacher in the surviving Ferrari hovered in third place. Frentzen's car was running lighter than David's, Williams having decided to stop twice for fuel, McLaren just once. Heinz-Harald

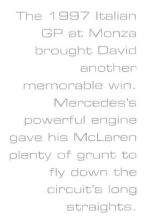

The 1997 Italian GP at Monza brought David another memorable win. Mercedes's powerful engine gave his McLaren plenty of grunt to fly down the circuit's long straights.

pulled away in the lead until lap 18, when he made his first stop. His margin had been 16 seconds – not enough to come into and out of the pits without giving up the lead. He rejoined in third place, behind Schumacher (second), and David, who was surprising his team with the speed he was able to maintain. In the McLaren garage and on the pit wall the realisation was dawning that this was a race they could win.

David was still leading when he came in on lap 32 for his only scheduled stop. Schumacher had stopped three laps earlier, dropping him to fifth, so David quickly found himself back in second, behind Frentzen. David was 'fuelled to the flag' as the vernacular has it; Frentzen had to stop once more to take on enough fuel to reach the finish. His lead over DC after David's first stop was 19 seconds. As Frentzen approached the pits for his second stop on lap 39 it was only 26 seconds.

Williams mechanics assumed their familiar positions for the pit stop routine. They knew that any mistake would delay their man long enough to let Coulthard sneak through into the lead and then Frentzen would have to pass David to win – a tall order on such a tight circuit, even with a faster car. In a moment's hesitation is a race won and lost. The mechanics changing the

Williams's right rear wheel had difficulty removing it. Five seconds slipped by … as did Coulthard and Schumacher, on track, into first and second places. David was a scant two seconds ahead of Schumacher – only just out of the danger zone of an improvised attack. Frentzen, having left the pits, was five seconds further back in third, but gaining each lap in the fastest car on the circuit. There were 18 laps of this to go. On the pit wall Ron Dennis was serene, informing his driver of the gap to Schumacher, telling him what he had to do, that everything was under control. On the track, in the heat of battle, in the sweltering cockpit, with emotion fuelling his adrenalin, David had to keep cool. Only a calm head would keep him ahead of Schumacher and Frentzen.

And then … release. Ferrari had miscalculated the amount of fuel Michael would need to complete the race. On lap 51 he was called into the pits for a splash of gas that would see him through to the finish. Still there was a threat from Frentzen, but on lap 56 it exploded in a shower of carbon fibre fragments. The Williams's left front brake disc had failed completely and Frentzen was sent spinning into the gravel.

David and Michael cruised the final two laps to the flag, 20 seconds separating the winner from second place. Mika Häkkinen finished third, only two seconds behind Michael but never having been in a position to threaten him. McLaren had both drivers on the podium. Their joy was complete.

The ecstasy of victory was clear to see in David's eyes as he pressed himself up from the cockpit. He pulled off his helmet and tore away his balaclava. His normally composed features were taut with emotion as the reality of his achievement sank in. All he could see ahead of him were ranks of smiling faces. The whole team, it seemed, had rushed to the winners' enclosure, *parc fermé*, to greet their conquering hero.

Soon he was on the top step of the podium, dewy-eyed and blinking in disbelief at the adulation being accorded this famous victory. His win had been a

Celebrations in the McLaren-Mercedes motorhome were unrestrained. David gets a 'beer shower' from Mercedes boss Norbert Haug. Haug had long championed Coulthard within the team and was delighted to see him win . . .

. . . just at that moment it looked as if the sky was the limit for David.

battle, far more than had his first, for Williams, 18 months earlier. The satisfaction in its achievement was all the greater. There was the added, unspoken, delight of having put one over his team-mate. As David stepped down from the top step of the podium, he was the golden boy dressed in silver. Ron Dennis was on the podium balcony, too – his privilege as a member of the winning team – and he could scarcely contain his delight. He hugged David, and placed a hand around the back of his head, drawing him closer. His eyes spoke of the sheer joy he was experiencing. Rarely have a driver and team principal looked closer.

Jo Ramirez recalls the afternoon (and the night that followed…) as one of the most unforgettable of his 18 years at McLaren. 'It had been 49 races since we had won, and you know, that was an unbelievable length of time for a team like us who had grown so used to winning. When Ayrton won at Adelaide in 1993, if people had said to me then, "It will be 49 races until you win again", I'd have said, "Go away, you're crazy." But there we were in the garage worrying that it was going to be 50 races since we had won and then maybe 51, 52, who knows.'

Before the race Jo had taken David quietly to one side in the garage and told him 'You have to win this one,' half joking, half imploring. 'Jo, I promise I'll do my best,' David had replied. 'When he won it was just

unbelievable. You cannot believe the tension in the garage for the whole race. It wasn't like it was an easy win, you know, with no one to fight. He was battling the whole way. I was the first up to him when he stepped out of the car. All I could say was, "You did it! You did it!" All he could say was, "I know! I know!" It was a beautiful moment.'

McLaren partied that night like it was their last win on earth, not the first of a new era. There had, however, been a few logistical problems to overcome first. The team had not expected to win the race and no celebratory meal had been arranged. All had expected to be getting the long-haul flight home after a solid weekend's work – not leaving the paddock with heads held high after an against-the-odds win.

Jo recalls: 'David was so happy. We were also happy, of course, but we had nothing prepared to celebrate. George Harrison came by, he had come to Melbourne and was a good friend of ours – one of the boys, really – and he wanted to join the party. He even offered to buy the champagne, but we didn't know what we were doing. Later, when we were trying to sort things out, I tried to call him at the Melbourne Hyatt. I knew he was staying there but reception wouldn't put me through because they were trying to protect him. So George was in danger of missing the party. Eventually I convinced them to put me through and I told George to come and find us in the Crown Towers Hotel in the middle of town. We were all glad he did: he ended up at five in the morning entertaining us with a song dedicated to Bernie. He was on great form because he and DC were good friends.'

It was an expensive night, particularly so for Norbert Haug, who had agreed to foot the bill. But David, too, was about to blow a hole in his wallet. At the end of '96 he had bet Ron Dennis £1 that he would not wear a kilt to the *Autosport* Awards dinner held at London's Grosvenor Hotel. Dennis accepted the bet, on the condition that David pay £24,999 to the Tommy's foetal health charity on the day that he won his first race for McLaren. The jovial relations between the two men seemed to give the lie to the frequent observation that Häkkinen was Dennis's favourite and that David would always have to fight for his boss's affections.

A little over a year earlier, a few months after joining McLaren, David had offered his thoughts on how he felt about his new boss: 'We've had plenty of time to get to know each other and he is obviously a different personality to Frank Williams. But I'm not going to say pleasant things at the moment, because it is only when you get to a real pressure situation that you truly find out if you work together and if you carry one another on to claim victories in the future.'[1] The pressure in Melbourne had been real enough, as had the win. But the ability to carry each other would prove elusive. It was not until the Canadian Grand Prix in June, three months later, that David's McLaren looked like winning again.

By now Adrian Newey had agreed to join McLaren, for a salary estimated to be $2 million a year. He had shown his face with his new team at Monaco but his input into the '97 chassis would be limited. His influence on the outcome of the '98 World Championship, however, would be very significant indeed. That was all to come. For now, McLaren and David were still intent on dragging the team into contention for the '97 title. The car had shown its speed, with both drivers regularly running near the front of the pack. But it lacked consistency – David and Mika were qualifying anywhere between the fifth and second rows, as they travelled from circuit to circuit.

In Montreal they appeared to have cracked it. David was fifth on the grid, and from there the race surrendered to him – until lap 51. At that point he appeared to be heading for a serene victory. He had taken the lead on lap 28 and, planning to make only one stop against Michael Schumacher's two, he should have been able to stroll to his second win of the season. But tyre problems were about to ruin his day. He had come into the pits on lap 39, as planned. Twelve laps later he was in again. Blisters on his tyres were spoiling the car's handling, so, with a 30-second lead, he was called in again. There was time for David to pit without losing the lead, if all went smoothly. The tyre change was swift enough, but as David attempted to accelerate from his garage the car stalled. Clutch problems prevented it from getting away. The car lurched forward, stalled. Lurched again, stalled again. Finally David got away, but in those wasted seconds the complexion of the race had changed.

Out on track, Olivier Panis, driving a Prost, had suffered a huge accident, his car smashing into tyre

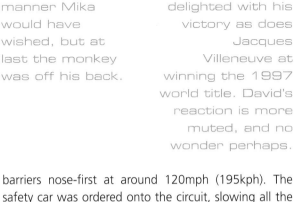

Jerez 1997. David gets the call from the pits asking him to move over and let Häkkinen through for his first F1 win. The victory may not have come in quite the manner Mika would have wished, but at last the monkey was off his back.

Häkkinen looks almost as delighted with his victory as does Jacques Villeneuve at winning the 1997 world title. David's reaction is more muted, and no wonder perhaps.

barriers nose-first at around 120mph (195kph). The safety car was ordered onto the circuit, slowing all the drivers behind it. David was now in seventh place, out of the points and unable to progress. As the drivers circulated slowly in strict line-astern order, safety crews worked to release Panis, who was stuck in the car with both his lower legs broken. It was two months before he could drive again, although he went on to make a full recovery.

Two laps later, with Panis still stricken, the race was stopped and the result declared. Michael Schumacher won, David had nothing to show for an impressive weekend. If he had stayed out of the pits one lap longer the race would have been his. This was sheer misfortune, and David later confided to a McLaren colleague: 'I must have done something really terrible in a previous life to have that sort of bad luck.'

It was the last thing he needed, as rumours swept the paddock that either he or Häkkinen would be replaced for '98. Moves were being made by West and Mercedes to find room for a German driver, the better to dovetail with their marketing plans. There was talk, too, that Damon Hill might join. In the event all the gossip came to nothing – both drivers re-signed in

August – but the pressure both were under to succeed was being bluntly expressed.

Mika had his own 'Canada' at Silverstone, where his engine blew while he was leading with seven laps to go. Other promising positions were squandered through unreliability or bad luck. McLaren's potential was clear to see; results and goodwill were in short supply.

Come the Italian Grand Prix at Monza, in September, the team's supply of 'success oxygen' was becoming increasingly stale. One win out of the first 12 races for an organisation so well funded and resourced was a poor return. There should have been four or five wins by now and the team should have been pushing at the head of the constructors' table rather than languishing in fourth place. David admitted as much in conversation, but there was also the sense that with his contract settled and the prospect of an Adrian Newey-designed car to drive in '98, his thoughts were already drifting to next year. 'I see absolutely no reason why we can't start '98 with an advantage over the opposition and at the very least be the most competitive out there. But of course I want the unfair advantage. I want a quicker car. I want all that.'[2]

Until then he would have to fight for his wins. At Monza, a track which rewards a car with a strong engine, David felt confident of his ability to challenge. Practice was mediocre, netting sixth place behind Häkkinen, whose lap was seven-thousandths of a second faster. In their intra-team battle it edged Mika ahead in the qualifying stakes, 6–7. They could hardly be closer. At the start David played his ace: his ability to gain positions off the line. This skill, which had been apparent since his earliest days in single-seaters, would regularly gain him in a few seconds what might otherwise take 20 or 30 laps to achieve.

Today was no different. From sixth, he went into the first corner third, behind Jean Alesi and Heinz-Harald Frentzen. 'I concentrated, focused, and got away superbly,' he said. Then he played a waiting game until the first round of pit stops, keeping Alesi and Frentzen within reach, but looking after his car and tyres. When the pit stops came, on lap 32, Alesi and David were running one-two, Frentzen having slipped back with an earlier stop. David was right behind Alesi as they entered the pits; the McLaren crew were nine-tenths of a second faster than the Benetton mechanics. In a breath the lead of the race had changed. David left the pits ahead of Alesi and he knew that barring incident, the win would be his. Twenty-one laps later, it was.

The euphoria of Melbourne was absent, but in its own way this race was as important for the McLaren-Mercedes partnership as had been the Australian GP. Momentum was being established; McLaren felt like a team on the up.

Two weeks later at the Austrian Grand Prix, Mika Häkkinen led before retiring at the end of the first lap, and David finished second. The MP4-12 had been fitted with a new front wing, fresh from the computer screens of Adrian Newey. It bore a remarkable similarity to that on the front of the Williams cars, which Newey had also designed. It was apparent at the next round, the Luxembourg Grand Prix at the Nürburgring circuit, that the McLaren's Newey-tuned aerodynamics had released the chassis' latent potential. They were the fastest cars at the circuit all weekend. Häkkinen took his first ever pole position and they dominated the race in first and second until lap 43, when David's engine blew. Mika's went just a lap later.

Despite the frustration of a double non-finish this was the sort of weekend from which a team can still take satisfaction. While the reliability was shaky, McLarens were the fastest cars on the track. Mika spoke of the new-found confidence he had in the car's handling and of how much he enjoyed working with Adrian Newey. Some believed his words were ominous, for Mika and David had always made different demands of their cars' handling. 'It was usually the case that year,' says one McLaren engineer, 'that when Mika was happy David felt less comfortable. When David was happy, Mika felt the car wasn't working for him. In the first half of '97, before Adrian joined us, it seemed to vary from one race to the next who would get the best out of the car. But when Adrian came along Mika's driving style was better for what he was designing. It boosted his confidence tremendously.'

What Newey had done, essentially, was to give the MP4-12 more front-end grip through better aerodynamic performance from its front wing. Häkkinen's style was very dependent on having a 'hard' front end, which he could point where he wanted. That created a tendency for the rear of the car to feel less stable, but this 'oversteer' characteristic suited his natural instincts. Unfortunately for David, it went precisely counter to his own need for a 'softer' front end.

For all his efforts and success throughout '97, the centre of gravity at McLaren was shifting. He and Mika had been incredibly closely matched all year, with David emerging ahead on points. He had been able to put to one side the suspicion that Ron Dennis would always be closer to Mika with on-track performances that demanded his boss's respect. But even outsiders could sense a change of atmosphere. One source close to the team says: 'David had been doing exceptionally well that year, but by mid '97 the honeymoon period was over. In any technical discussions Ron would come in and focus entirely on Mika. David felt pushed to one side.'

At the Japanese Grand Prix, the penultimate race of the year, David found himself unable to 'balance' his car to his liking and he was not given use of the most powerful Mercedes engine for qualifying. Then came

Jerez, the final race of the season and the stage for what would prove to be a dramatic championship decider for protagonists Jacques Villeneuve and Michael Schumacher.

History records that Jacques finished third and won the title, having survived an attempt by Schumacher to barge him off the track. The move cost Michael his second position in the race and later, after an investigation by the governing body, his second position in the championship (although he was allowed to keep his individual race results).

Such was the drama of this bitter twist to the finale, Mika Häkkinen's first win was almost overlooked. He and David had run right behind Villeneuve in the early stages and their proximity to Jacques suggested they had the speed to pass him. They held back. Their 'generosity' was repaid later when Jacques, leading the latter stages of the race and on his way to the world title after Schumacher's retirement, pulled over to let the two McLarens past. With Schumacher already out, third position would guarantee him the championship.

It later emerged that Williams and McLaren had reached an accommodation whereby the McLarens held back early on, so as not to interfere with the Villeneuve-Schumacher showdown. Lap 68, when Jacques relinquished the race lead, was payback time.

Had there ever been a happier winner than Mika Häkkinen? After 96 races, he had finally taken his first grand prix victory. For David it was a more bittersweet moment. He had run ahead of Mika after the first pit stops but was ordered to pull over and let Mika though on lap 66, just three from the end. A race win he felt should have been his was gifted to Häkkinen.

A little later a couple of trusted journalists found David around the back of the McLaren trucks. He was seething, still sweating, his face screwed up with anger and frustration. 'I hate this. I *hate* this.'

The result mattered little in the context of the championship, for David still finished third to Mika's fifth. But the confidence boost that first win gave to Häkkinen was immeasurable, as a watching world was about to find out.

[1] *Autosport*, 14 December 1995.

[2] *Autosport*, 4 September 1997.

Many have made the mistake of believing David 'too nice' to win in F1. This study of his focus, determination, and anger might convince them otherwise.

David's win at the 1997 Australian Grand Prix had been one of the sweetest of his career. A year later events took a darker turn.

help!

'I think Ron could have been just as close to David as he became to Mika but maybe Mika played a clever game. They developed a tremendous rapport after Mika's accident.' This is the opinion of a well-placed McLaren source who worked closely with all three men in the late 1990s. During that time he gained a clear insight into the relationships between them and watched as the team's subconscious bias shifted towards Häkkinen after his first win, at Jerez, in '97. Thereafter, David's position was eroded. Not in any crass way – the drivers' cars were always prepared to the same standard and both could call on first-rate engineers. But in terms of McLaren's internal functioning, David's influence lessened as the team looked to Mika to bring wins and championships.

'At the start of '97, when DC won the first race, everything was really quite cool,' the source says. 'But after DC had to give Mika his first win at Jerez, Mika started to win all the time. As he had nearly died in one of Ron's cars there was inevitably some sort of bond between them and because everybody talked about it, it became more of a reality. It was almost a self-fulfilling prophecy. Everybody started to say Mika was the favourite son and whether that was true or not, within the team, people started to believe it.'

McLaren veteran Jo Ramirez believes Coulthard and Dennis may, in fact, be too similar in certain aspects of their character ever to become truly close. 'They are both tough people. DC has a very strong character and very strongly believes in himself and what he thinks. I remember in his first or second year with us, he was

having trouble handling an oversteering car. Mika, of course, was comfortable in a car like that, but David couldn't get on with it. He was losing it and having a few spins and couldn't get the car to his liking. At one point we sent him to Paul Ricard for a three-day test dedicated solely to getting the car the way he wanted it. It was all arranged just for him by Ron and we went through all the changes, tried everything he asked for.

'Unfortunately David didn't make a point of thanking Ron for arranging the test and Ron was hurt that DC didn't say thank you. He had spent probably the equivalent of £50,000 over those three days, maybe more, and DC didn't call him. Unfortunately for David, Ron remembers things like that. I'm sure it was just an oversight on David's part, and if he had thought about it I think he would have seen the value of spending 10p to call Ron. He would do it now, I think. Little things like that didn't help the relationship.'

The 1998 Australian Grand Prix at Melbourne underlined the doubts of those who believed Coulthard would never flourish at McLaren as long as Häkkinen remained there. Mika and David had qualified one-two, Mika on pole, just four-thousandths of a second ahead. Their new McLaren MP4-13, with a Mercedes engine and Bridgestone tyres, had a clear performance advantage over all its rivals. It had been designed by Adrian Newey, in accordance with new regulations intended to reduce cornering speeds: the cars were narrower and their slick tyres were grooved to reduce grip. It was the first all-Newey McLaren and it was a gem. So good was it that Mika and David had agreed that whichever of them was ahead into the first corner would not be challenged by his team-mate. That meant they were, in effect, deciding who would win the race. The car had been so fast in testing and was so fleet during the qualifying sessions, it seemed a certain winner – provided it was reliable. MP4-13 had been developed late and McLaren had not carried out as much pre-season testing as they would have liked. That did not prevent David and Mika from dominating practice, but they would not race hard once the sprint to the first corner was over.

'I was confident of beating Mika away at the start,' David said later. 'The deal seemed like a good idea at the time, but they held us an awful long time on the grid and I was distracted by smoke beginning to come from my radiators. I made a very average start which was a real bummer in the circumstances.' He gained no advantage into turn one and the outcome was sealed. No one else knew of their agreement; all that was apparent was that two gorgeous McLarens were dominating in a manner not seen since the Senna-Prost days. When they came in for their first pit stops they were a minute and 14 seconds ahead of Jacques Villeneuve in third.

They emerged Mika first, David second, even before Villeneuve came in for his first stop. So it would have remained to the flag, had it not been for an error from Häkkinen on lap 36. Mika misheard a call from his pits, because of a slight hearing problem that had afflicted him since his Adelaide '95 accident. He believed, incorrectly, he had been told to come into the pits and pulled in four laps too early. As he arrived at the team garage, he found none of the pit crew were ready for him. All he could do was drive through, waving his arms in frustration. The confusion had cost him the lead. He came in again four laps later, David two laps after that, and they emerged David first, Mika second, with more than a minute in hand over their nearest challenger, Heinz-Harald Frentzen.

For 13 more laps David ran serenely ahead of his team-mate until, on lap 55, he slowed suddenly on the pit straight to let Mika through. Cynics cried 'foul', believing David had once again fallen victim to favouritism for Häkkinen. But no, David said later, his move was simply a means of honouring the pre-race agreement in the light of Mika's being artificially hampered by his dud pit stop. Ron Dennis insisted, too, that the decision had been David's: 'It was not a team order, it was David's decision after the team made a mistake in calling in Mika for a pit stop.'

David's corporate face remained fixedly in place during the post-race press conference, but at least one close friend believes the truth of the situation is somewhat different: 'David was as angry as he had been after Jerez in '97, but he had to keep a lid on it "for the good of the team". In his view, Mika had made a mistake and should have been made to live with the consequences. He couldn't believe he had been made to give up the win. Both situations were completely unjustifiable, appalling really, but David's honeymoon period with the team had been over for a long time by then. Almost from day one Ron would walk straight past David in team briefings and start talking to Mika about the car. It was Ron talking to Mika on the pit wall, never to David.'

David pulls to the left of the main straight at Melbourne's Albert Park in 1998, to allow Häkkinen past. The move was viewed with deep cynicism by the world's media and did nothing for David's relations with team management.

Aggrieved he may have been, but David still had the compensation of knowing he was driving a car capable of winning the World Championship. For the first time since '95 he could look forward to a season in a machine with a performance advantage over its opposition. This was his best chance yet of becoming World Champion. Except that in Mika Häkkinen he faced a team-mate as fast and determined as any other on the planet. In terms of pure speed only Michael Schumacher was Mika's equal, but there were many, both inside and outside the team, who felt David could beat him over a season.

London-based *F1 Racing* magazine nailed its colours to David's mast early in the season, declaring on the cover of its May '98 issue that 'Coulthard could humble Häkkinen'. The magazine contained a hefty essay by respected F1 journalist Peter Windsor – a long-time admirer of Coulthard – arguing David's case, and a leader column by editor Matt Bishop reinforcing Windsor's opinion. Bishop's editorial, however, maintained that while David could prevail, Häkkinen remained the faster driver.

The San Marino Grand Prix at Imola followed the publication of the May '98 issue and Bishop travelled to the race in good spirits, believing it would sell well to its British readers and also that it had been appropriately supportive of Britain's leading driver. David did not see things that way. Soon after entering the Imola paddock he confronted Bishop.

'I wasn't expecting any grief at all,' Bishop says, 'but I was wrong. David walked up to me and began berating me politely but very firmly. There was a bit of finger wagging too, and he criticised the leader column I had written for being "not helpful". He was very disappointed but I remember feeling somewhat aggrieved because the cover and the inside package were incredibly positive for him.' (Accurate, too. David won the San Marino GP – his first win of the year, after back-to-back Häkkinen victories in Australia and Brazil, followed by a first win for Michael Schumacher in Argentina.)

The story is notable not only for illustrating the fact that David reads his press – uncommon for a Formula 1 driver – but also that he is sensitive enough to be hurt, or buoyed, by what is written about him. It is a

characteristic at odds with the studied insouciance of his public manner, but friends and colleagues are familiar with a degree of Coulthard delicacy.

Anna Guerrier, McLaren's head of press and PR from '96 to 2000, believes his intelligence and analytical nature leave him exposed to barbs: 'He's quite a sensitive guy and if somebody had written something that he felt was particularly unfair he might get a bit annoyed about it. Jacques Villeneuve is the sort of guy who might just punch someone in the paddock if he was angry, but David's not like that at all. Can you imagine him doing that? He's a really sensitive, sensible, intelligent individual who just happens to be a Formula 1 driver.'

The suggestion that David may be an innocent abroad amid the swirl of F1 paddock politics is recurrent among those who have worked with him. His racing ability is rarely called into question, but the observation that he may be 'too nice for his own good' has been made repeatedly. 'Mika knew it, too,' says

one McLaren source, 'and he played on it in a very subtle psychological way. He would come across as this monosyllabic Finn, but not because he had nothing to say – he was far too intelligent for that.'

David, ever the loyal company man, and a character of essential decency, would confide to those he trusted that he was sometimes flummoxed by the apparent inarticulacy of his team-mate, which left him to shoulder McLaren's PR burden at a time when he would rather have been debriefing with his engineers. There seemed little alternative, however. It was a further complication in the already baffling task of how to get on terms with a team-mate whose momentum became increasingly irresistible throughout '98.

David won only once that year while Mika took the chequered flag eight times, along with six fastest laps and nine pole positions. Häkkinen had put together a virtuoso season to become World Champion. He led the championship from start to finish; only at the Italian GP at Monza did his title

rival Michael Schumacher draw level on 80 points, before Mika pulled away once more over the last two races. The statistics still look painful for David, but behind the results table is a story of dutiful support for a team-mate McLaren had decided by mid-season would spearhead their world title challenge.

David's car had been the less reliable of the two in the first half of the season, costing him heavy points scores in Monaco and Canada, then, later in the year, at the Italian GP. By the time of the British GP at Silverstone, the decision had been taken that David would drive to support Mika's title campaign, as the threat from Michael Schumacher's Ferrari became more intense.

Riding shotgun goes against every instinct that makes a racing driver a competitive sportsman, but at the end of the year David attempted to explain how he had kept a rein on his ambition. 'People who have never been in the situation in which I found myself this year naturally find it difficult to understand why any

racing driver would give away a win, for example. After all, they'll say, a real racer would never do that. The reality is the championship represents everything we are racing for as a team. Going against a request to move over would be a quick way out of it. I've had the chance to drive for the best team, but in any case you need an engine and you need a car. Supporting Mika meant that gradually I slipped back to third place in the championship, but it was important to work for him and for the team.'[1]

Of the many good turns done by David for Mika that year, none was more dramatic – or unintended – than his clash with Michael Schumacher at the Belgian Grand Prix, which put both out of the race. Spa, as so often, was drenched. The rivalry between Häkkinen and Schumacher was becoming ever more acute, as Ferrari regained some of the ground they had lost to McLaren early in the season. Their respective team-mates, Coulthard and Eddie Irvine, were also fast and competitive, while the Jordan pairing of Damon Hill and Ralf Schumacher were edging closer to the pace, as were the Williams and Benetton teams. The weekend was becoming one of F1's occasional pressure points, where the intensity of competition is such that something has to give – particularly when there was the added unpredictability of a wet track.

So it proved. Moments after the start David lost control of his car coming out of the La Source hairpin. McLaren number seven spun, clipped a barrier and bounced across the track, forcing those behind to dive left and right in avoidance. The inevitable accident was of monstrous scale. Twelve cars ran into each other, or off the track: Coulthard's McLaren, Eddie Irvine's Ferrari, two Prost cars, two Arrows, two Tyrrells, Rubens Barrichello's Stewart, Johnny Herbert's Sauber, the Benetton of Alex Wurz, and Shinji Nakano's Minardi. Pieces of bent and broken Formula 1 car covered the track like autumn leaves. The race was stopped immediately as the teams took stock of the carnage. No drivers were seriously hurt, but Rubens Barrichello had bumped an elbow and decided not to take the restart. Three other drivers were left without cars as their team-mate had taken the spare.

The second start came an hour later, the track still streaming. Damon Hill led in the Jordan, ahead of title protagonists Häkkinen and Schumacher. Mika and Michael touched at the first corner, forcing Mika into a spin and retirement. Less than a lap later David spun as well, and while he was able to carry on, he was running last. Light rain continued to fall, keeping the track moist and restricting the drivers' visibility as their cars' tyres raised clouds of spray.

Schumacher had by now pushed Hill down to second place and was leading by half a minute. He came up to lap David on their 25th tour. Even by his standards Schumacher had been driving with particular aggression in Belgium. Before attempting to pass David he waved his arm out of the cockpit, as if to make him move over. As the pair went nose-to-tail towards the sweeping Pouhon corner, David edged to the right and lifted off the throttle to let Michael through. The move surprised Schumacher and his Ferrari slammed into the McLaren at 137mph (220kph) – the precise speed revealed by Ferrari technical director Ross Brawn – ripping off the red car's right front wheel and nose wing. The McLaren's rear wing was also torn off. The

Coulthard and *F1 Racing* editor Matt Bishop have a frank exchange at the 1998 San Marino GP. An article published in *F1 Racing* before the race had been 'unhelpful' in David's eyes, and he let Bishop know what he thought!

pair continued to the pits, Michael's three-wheeler providing one of the images of the year. Schumacher was raging. As he parked up, he tore off his belts and stormed along the pit lane to the McLaren garage, face dark as thunder. Ferrari team principal Jean Todt scuttled after him, trying to pull Michael back, but his driver broke away, intent on 'getting even' with DC.

McLaren team co-ordinator Jo Ramirez was standing next to David as Schumacher strode towards them. 'I just couldn't believe it,' he says, 'DC didn't do anything wrong. Michael was completely over the top. He was shouting "You tried to kill me! You tried to kill me!" As far as I was concerned the accident was totally Michael's fault. He drove into the back of DC, after all. He was driving beyond his means. There was no way he could do what he was trying to do. The top drivers do tend to take more risks and Michael took a big risk there. He was driving beyond his vision and he really hit DC.

'He stormed into the garage like a man possessed. He was full of adrenalin. I couldn't believe what I was seeing. He was convinced that DC had lifted off purposely to cause the accident. Michael was really out of control when he came into the garage. His race

engineer Stefano Domenicali had to haul him away. DC was astonished. He didn't think what Michael was saying was possible.'

Talking about the incident five years later, DC was asked who would have won a fist-fight if a scuffle had broken out, as had looked likely. 'I think I would have won on the basis that I still had my crash helmet on. His first punch would have broken his hand and then I would have "used the heed" [sic] and given him a Glasgow Kiss. Easy!'

At the 2003 French Grand Prix, however, David admitted that lifting off the throttle as he had, while still on the racing line, was not the most prudent course of action. 'When Michael ran into the back of me, his reaction was that I'd "brake-tested" him or tried to kill him and all that sort of thing. The stewards looked at the data and I hadn't braked, so it was all just brushed under the carpet. The reality is that I lifted to let him pass me, but I lifted in heavy spray on the racing line. You should never do that. I would never do that now. In 1998, I didn't have the experience and the knowledge, and I had never had someone run into the back of me. And because someone pushes you, you

David relaxing in his motorhome, in which he stays at all European Grands Prix. Unusually for an F1 driver, he reads the motorsport press avidly – as editors have found to their cost from time to time . . .

react. So you act as though "I didn't do that". The minute I knew he was there, and was trying to pass me, I should have made a smarter decision.'

'Smart' or not, David's actions had prevented Schumacher from gaining ten points on Häkkinen on a day when Mika did not score. Ferrari fans never forgave him. At the next race, the Italian Grand Prix at Monza, 'Killer Coulthard' signs were draped from safety fences, and some fans spat at him as he walked back to the pits after retiring from a ten-second lead on lap 17. David returned the compliments with theatrical bows to the grandstands. It was another trying episode in a tough year for David, one whose rewards did not equal the effort expended.

The same could not be said for Häkkinen, who six weeks later sealed the title at the Japanese Grand Prix. As he and David stepped from their cars in *parc fermé*, after finishing first and third, he said to his team-mate: 'Next year it's you'. David, who finished a distant third in the championship, with 56 points to Mika's 100, could only hope he was right. Most pundits, however, reckoned '99 would bring more of the same. McLaren

Retirements at the Monaco and Canadian Grands Prix cost DC's title hopes dear. The 1998 McLaren was an absolute gem, but where Häkkinen used it to go from strength to strength (and a world title), David was frustrated by poor reliability.

The 1998 Belgian Grand Prix was one of the most dramatic in F1 history. A huge accident at the start was followed by a clash between Schumacher and David after the re-start. Michael lost a wheel in the shunt, but sped back to the pits to confront David...

and Ferrari were leaving their driver pairings unchanged (Häkkinen-Coulthard; Schumacher-Irvine) and their technical personnel were largely stable. In addition both teams would run on Bridgestone tyres, removing one performance variable. Competition between the two was therefore likely to be even closer.

And so it proved over a season full of thrills and incident. Once again the title fight went to the last race, at Suzuka, but once again it was the Häkkinen McLaren in the vanguard and the Coulthard machine left trailing in its exhaust fumes. In contrast to '98, however, David had been in the thick of the title fight until all but the last two rounds.

He travelled to round 14 – the European Grand Prix, at the Nürburgring – with 48 points, trailing Jordan's Heinz-Harald Frentzen on 50, and Irvine and Häkkinen both on 60. Michael Schumacher's season had been wrecked by an accident at the British Grand Prix ten weeks earlier. A fracture to his right leg put him out for six races and out of contention for the championship. David, meanwhile,

knew he had a good shot at the title, as 'team orders' had not been brought into play at McLaren.

When Ron Dennis was quizzed before the race on the subject of whether or not David might be 'asked' to drive in support of Häkkinen, he said: 'For 15 years our contracts have allowed the drivers to get on with it. We feel competent at assessing a situation in the race and taking a view on it. In certain circumstances we would ask one driver to allow another to pass; if these circumstances arise we will do it.' Translation: they have not arisen yet; David would not be expected to play a supporting role to Mika.

From the beginning of practice in Germany David drove with exceptional vigour. He out-qualified Häkkinen for only the second time that year (P2 to Mika's P3) and ran a strong third in the first quarter of the race. He enjoyed a little luck on lap 20, when Häkkinen, ahead of him, was called into the pits to change to wet tyres. Almost as soon as he rejoined, the light rain, which had made one side of the circuit

slippery, stopped. Mika was forced back into the pits for new dry tyres and he resumed in 14th place, knowing he would be lucky to pick up a point. Irvine, too, had fallen victim to a pit lane gaffe and was also running down the order, just one place ahead of Häkkinen. David and Frentzen, running second and first, were poised to haul themselves to the very tip of the sharp end of the title fight.

Then, disaster for Frentzen. Pulling out of the pits after his first stop on lap 32, his car's electrics died. Things were suddenly looking very good indeed for David. He had won earlier in the year in Britain and Belgium. Win number three was his for the taking. On a wet-dry track he was pulling away from Ralf Schumacher's Williams at around two seconds a lap. Maybe he was trying too hard, for on lap 38 he spun, nudged a tyre barrier, and retired. The championship chance which he had seemed to be holding firmly between both hands had been fumbled and allowed to fall.

David knew what he had lost, and was ruthlessly self-critical in confessing all to journalist David Tremayne at the end of the season: 'I comprehensively fucked it up there. I was really disappointed when I went back to the motorhome. Mika and Eddie were out of contention. I was leading and pulling away in a difficult situation and at that moment I should have had the brainpower to hold myself back. Although I was getting instructions from the team to take it easy, I had already clicked myself into "You've got to push if you want to win this race." It was a mindset mistake. I have no one to blame other than myself.'[2]

David was right to rue his error, for he had been a far more convincing challenger to Häkkinen throughout '99. At Imola, round three, he led strongly and should have won the race, but was badly held up by Prost driver Olivier Panis, whom he was trying to lap. Four races later, in France, David led again, passing early leader Barrichello and pulling away 'as if in a different race', according to one observer, only to retire on lap ten with a failed alternator. He won the next race, the

Post-Suzuka 1998, Häkkinen tells David: 'Next year, it's you.' The sentiment may have been genuine, but McLaren's support seemed to remain firmly behind Mika into 1999.

British Grand Prix at Silverstone, with an emphatic performance. He had been confident all weekend and held off race-long pressure from Irvine. This was the event, of course, at which Michael Schumacher broke his right leg, while Häkkinen also retired, after a wheel hub failure.

The performances of the McLaren pair were close and the 'edge' between them glinted at Austria, where they touched at the second corner, causing Mika to spin. The contact wasn't deliberate, but colliding with a team-mate is the cardinal sin for a Formula 1 driver: 'Thou shalt not…'

David was contrite afterwards: 'It was my nightmare scenario – taking my own team-mate off on the first lap.' At least, he *appeared* contrite. He revealed quietly a year later that while he professed *mea culpa* at the time, he believes the fault lay with Mika. 'I was in front, Mika was behind. He tried to pass and we crashed. I have a contract with the team and I accepted responsibility. It was only to calm everyone. But it was certainly not the truth.'[3]

As Mika Häkkinen went from success to success in 1998, David could feel the team's centre of gravity shifting away from him. Häkkinen found Adrian Newey's cars suited his driving style better than they did David's. DC managed only one win and struggled to remain in touch with Mika, whose confidence grew by the race.

This 'off' at the 1999 European GP cost David any chance of winning the world title. At the end of the season he was still regretting the slip, saying he had pushed too hard for the conditions without realising he could have backed off.

Three races later, at Spa, David again attacked Häkkinen forcefully. Mika had qualified ahead of David, but started poorly, allowing David to nose ahead as they ran down to the first corner hairpin. Mika tried to hold the inside line and force David wide, but David's car was ahead and he could see his opportunity. After the briefest of touches between the silver cars – hardly more than a lovers' kiss – David was through and away, pulling out six-and-a-half seconds over the first ten laps. Häkkinen was unable to match David's pace and finished ten seconds down.

This second contact in a handful of races had enraged Häkkinen, however, and after the chequered flag he refused to shake his team-mate's hand. David consoled himself with subsequent comments from Ron Dennis, which vindicated his robust approach. Dennis declined to blame either driver for their coming-together, but, he added, David's reaction had been a natural response to Mika's slow start. Häkkinen's post-race mood betrayed some of the pressure he was under in trying to defend his title, and also some of his inner fragility – a rarely seen element of his complex character.

Mika splintered again three weeks later, at Monza, where he broke down in tears after making a mistake which threw away the lead and a certain ten points. The image of a crumpled, burdened champion-elect was appropriate for the season, for a thread of frustration ran though '99: Häkkinen could have taken the title earlier; Coulthard might have done, with more reliability; Irvine should have enjoyed more support from his team; Frentzen needed more luck.

No one could claim that Häkkinen was not a worthy champion, but he had made harder work of the title campaign than he should have. He scored 76 points to David's 48 and finished three places higher in the championship table. But both knew the figures hid the intensity of their struggle in '99; both knew things might be different in 2000.

[1] *Autosport*, 24/31 December 1998.

[2] *Autosport*, 6 December 1999.

[3] *F1 Racing*, August 2000.

More champagne at Monaco in 2000. The first of two wins at the most prestigious track of all. David was slightly lucky to benefit from the retirements of those ahead of him, but the joy of victory in Monte Carlo is clear to see.

yesterday

David Coulthard woke up on the morning of 3 May 2000 – a simple fact for which he will always be grateful. A day earlier David, his then-fiancée, Heidi Wichlinksi, and David's trainer Andy Matthew, survived a plane crash which killed the pilot and co-pilot – the only other people on board.

They had been flying from Farnborough, 35 miles south-west of London, to Nice, in the south of France. From take-off, flight NEX 4B was as routine a plane journey as David had ever made. He had not met the pilots, David Saunders and Dan Worley, before, as this particular aircraft, a twin-engined Learjet registered G-MURI, was not one on which he usually flew. It had been chartered from owner David Murray, chairman of Rangers football club. Exactly one hour after take-off, at 12.22pm, the plane's left engine failed at an altitude of 39,000 feet. The crew shut down the engine immediately and declared an emergency.[1] The flight was diverted to Lyon-Satolas airport, 62 miles (100km) away.

In the report into the incident by the French national accident investigation body, the BEA, the authors note: 'The descent, with one engine

There would be no looking back for David Coulthard in 2000. This would be a dramatic year in which he took three wins and emerged as a powerful threat to Michael Schumacher.

shut down, towards Lyon-Satolas was undertaken under radar guidance, at a high speed and with a high rate of descent.' In that sentence is hidden seventeen-and-a-half minutes of extreme duress. The report contains a transcript of the pilots' conversation, taken from the cockpit voice recorder, from the moment an engine problem was suspected, to the crash landing.

12h 20m 53s	*captain*	'Does that sound noisy to you?'
12h 20m 58s	*co-pilot*	'What, the radio?'
12h 20m 59s	*captain*	'No, the engine.'
12h 21m 40s	*captain*	'Hear that?'
12h 21m 55s	*captain*	'What is that?'
12h 21m 57s	*captain*	'It's the left engine, look, and the hyd…'
12h 22m 12s	*captain*	'Oh shit! We've lost it. Mayday. Mayday', accompanied by a fall in engine speed.
12h 22m 15s	*co-pilot to Bordeaux control*	'Mayday. Mayday. Mayday. Nex Four Bravo. We've lost an engine at flight level three nine zero and we're in the descent.'
12h 22m 30s	*captain*	'I'm shutting the left down.'
12h 23m 17s	*captain to Bordeaux control*	'Netax Four Bravo we also smell smoke in the cockpit – we need vectors to the nearest airfield.'
12h 24m 02s	*captain to Marseille control*	'We need the nearest airfield with 1600 metres Netax Four Bravo.'
12h 27m 00s	*captain*	'I don't. That other one's making funny noises.'
12h 27m 54s	*co-pilot*	'It's alright, Dave. I'll sort that out. Don't worry about that.'
12h 27m 57s	*co-pilot*	'Keep just keep it flying.'
12h 28m 43s	*captain*	'I don't like the sound of… I don't like that other vibration.'
12h 30m 13s	*captain*	'I don't like the sound of that other engine, that's why I'm worried.'
12h 30m 43s	*captain*	'Affirm this is a full emergency.'
12h 32m 24s	*captain*	'We should have a discrete frequency on a Mayday.'
12h 32m 46s	*captain*	'Tighten your seat belt.'
12h 32m 51s	*co-pilot*	'Twenty copied Nex Four Bravo.'

After his seemingly miraculous escape from a private plane crash, David was besieged by the world's media at the 2000 Spanish Grand Prix. McLaren helped him keep the journalists and photographers at bay.

12h 32m 52s	*co-pilot*	'Better start bringing the speed back now.'
12h 33m 13s	*captain*	'Just watch the indications on that good engine.'
12h 33m 15s	*captain*	'Keep your eyes open for the field.'
12h 33m 34s	*co-pilot*	'OK three to go high rate of descent.'
12h 36m 04s to 09s	*captain*	'There's two runways. There's two isn't... We're going for the left.'
12h 36m 19s	*captain*	'Can you tighten my seat belt?'
12h 36m 21s	*co-pilot*	'What do you want to do with it?'
12h 36m 21s	*captain*	'I think it what... it's that one isn't it? Oh shit, no.'
12h 36m 24s	*co-pilot*	'Want it... just tighten it.'
12h 36m 25s	*captain*	'Yeah, you know, you know, the lock.'
12h 36m 27s	*co-pilot*	'There you go.'
12h 36m 28s	*captain*	'Is it locked? That's it. Thanks. And yours?'
12h 37m 08s	*captain*	'Follow me through. Get rid of your paperwork and follow me through.'

12h 37m 47s	*captain*:	'On landing I'm going to stop the aeroplane.'
12h 38m 02s	*captain to Lyon tower*	'And two Bravo on landing we will exit all the passengers immediately.'
12h 38m 08.5s	*co-pilot*	'OK a little bit low, little bit low.'
12h 38m 12.8s	*co-pilot*	'You want all the flaps?'
12h 38m 12.8s	*captain*	'Not yet.'
12h 38m 17.7s	*co-pilot*	'Plus ten. You're getting a little bit low.'
12h 38m 20.8s	*co-pilot*	'Little bit low.'
12h 38m 22.2s	*captain*	'Oh shit.'
12h 38m 22.8s	*co-pilot*	'Little bit low.'
12h 38m 23.3s	*co-pilot*	'Put the power.'
12h 38m 23.45s	*captain*	'Shit.'
12h 38m 24s and 25s	*captain*	'I'm losing it.'
12h 38m 28s:	noise of impact.	
12h 38m 29s:	end of recording	

Seconds before the attempted landing the pilot increased the power through the right engine. The plane veered slightly to the left and rolled in the same direction. The left wing tip dropped and touched the Tarmac, dragging the aircraft around and pulling it nose-first into the ground. The cockpit was destroyed

in the impact, killing both pilots instantly. The fuselage, however, remained largely intact, although a fire broke out on the right-hand side of the aircraft, preventing David and his two fellow passengers from exiting through the emergency door. They fled, instead, through the gaping hole at the front of the fuselage. Heidi's Maltese terrier, Moody, which had been travelling with them, had already been thrown to safety through the hole by David, and was running around outside the plane, barking in distress.

The BEA report records: 'At one time the aircraft seemed to stop descending, its nose slightly up. At that moment the roll rate seemed constant to one of the observers. The closest observers heard a reduction in engine power before noticing a very rapid roll. Two heard a thrust increase before the aircraft's left tank touched the ground. The left wing touched the ground first, then the cockpit. When the aircraft came to a stop the right side caught fire. The firemen arrived as some people were coming out of the front of the aircraft.'

David, Heidi, and Andy Matthew were almost unscathed physically, although three of David's right-

There was joy at the British GP in 2000, where David took on, and beat, Häkkinen and Schumacher in a straight fight. Speaking after the race he said the win had been his best yet, and he seemed more confident than ever.

No love was lost between Michael Schumacher and David after a series of run-ins on the track over the years, and when David squeezed past at Magny-Cours, having been 'chopped' a lap earlier, he let Michael know what he thought of his driving standards...

hand ribs were cracked in the impact and he also suffered muscle damage. All three were taken to the Edouard-Herriot hospital in Lyon, but were released after a short examination.

It later emerged that a ball bearing failure had caused the shutdown of the left engine. The report also states that the Learjet was known to exhibit a marked turning characteristic when power was increased through only one of its engines. Experienced Learjet pilots knew control of the aircraft could easily be lost when 'powering up' on a single engine.

David's family were on holiday together in La Manga, Spain at the time of the accident. His sister Lynsay remembers receiving the call telling her what had happened: 'We were all having a nice afternoon playing pitch and putt in the sunshine. I picked up the mobile, heard what had happened, but then I was told immediately he was OK, so at that moment I wasn't that worried. But then an hour or so later we saw the first pictures on Sky News and I heard the poor pilots

had died. All I could think was "Oh my God". I really panicked then. It was pretty scary.

'I've never really spoken to him about it since because I didn't want to bring back bad memories. But the one question I did ask him at the time was "Did you get in the brace position?" He said "No, I got in the 'Get the Hell out of here position' – as far back as I could possibly be".'

Two days later David arrived at the Circuit de Catalunya, in Barcelona, to contest the Spanish Grand Prix. The media were restrained in their demands for comments on the ordeal and David appeared appreciative of the space he had been given. After surviving such a disturbing experience, he welcomed the barriers erected around the team by Ron Dennis. Instructions had been given to all employees that David should be offered whatever support he required this weekend, with the result that the media were kept at a marked distance.

The familiar isolation of a racing cockpit helped keep his mind from dwelling on trauma. He appeared more resolute, more determined than ever. He drove brilliantly. After holding a press conference in which he expressed his deepest sympathy for the pilots, but explained that he would be racing because that was what he had been born to do, he went on to vindicate his decision. He qualified fourth, finished second, having overcome a vigorously defensive Michael Schumacher. McLaren's second one-two of the year said much for the team's depth of ability and for David's steel.

'I firmly believe I will be a stronger person out of this,' he said later. 'It's a bit like before I had my first proper shunt in a GP car in a test session at Silverstone. Before that there is always the thought of the unknown. Everyone is like that. When we do not know something we are always a little bit cautious. Once you have had the big shunt you know what it's all about and can be confident about it. I felt stronger as a person then and I will do after this.'

At this early stage of the season, round five, David was lying third in the championship, two points behind Häkkinen but already 16 behind Schumacher. He had won McLaren's first race of the year, at

David analysed every detail of Häkkinen's performance over the winter of 2000/1, in an attempt to out-do his team-mate. They had been more evenly matched than ever in 2000 and David was convinced he could carry that form into 2001.

At Brazil in 2001 Juan Pablo Montoya's pass of Michael Schumacher brought fans to their feet. Forgotten in the excitement was David's arguably even better pass in worse conditions, to take the race lead and victory.

Silverstone, two weeks earlier, on a dank April weekend which called into question the future of the British Grand Prix there, so abject was the chaos in the circuit's muddied car parks.

Such matters were far from David's mind as he basked in a vodka-warmed, post-race glow, satisfied in the knowledge that he had beaten both Häkkinen and Schumacher. 'I suppose it might have been my best win,' he admitted.

There was an extra frisson to David's manner this year. Interviewers noticed a new intensity, an added impatience. The fine words David had always been able to muster were being matched by inner conviction. At Silverstone he had beaten Schumacher and Häkkinen on merit. In Spain he had performed at a level beyond what could ever have been expected.

Monaco brought another measured win, after out-qualifying his team-mate and driving patiently to pick up maximum points when others fell by the wayside. Something of the added dynamism his driving had acquired came through when he spoke of the strength he had felt at Monaco: 'Two drivers in front of me [Michael Schumacher and Jarno Trullli] retired and I was able to win. I felt incredibly strong. I was driving the

car, the car was not driving me. It's a very good memory.'[2] He was exploiting a car, the McLaren MP4-15, whose handling he was able to tune perfectly to his driving style; he was exploiting too, the first signs of Häkkinen 'battle fatigue'.

Both Mika's World Championships had been nerve-jangling affairs, squabbled over for a whole season and undecided until the final round. He entered 2000 within touching distance of an unprecedented title hat-trick, but after retirements at the first two races and a win only at round five, the path ahead looked uncertain at best. His thirst for the fray had anyway been diminished by his seasons in the sun.

When David won again, at the French Grand Prix, the victory tally between the McLaren drivers was 3–1 in David's favour. His old mentor, Jackie Stewart, ever the acute observer of driving talent, had noticed a change in David and could see a world title beckoning: 'He can win it,' said Stewart. 'I have noticed a difference in him in recent races. He has always been with top teams since he came into F1 and maybe that took a bit of the commitment and focus away, but now there is a realisation of what is at stake and what he can achieve this year. He is in a strong position.'

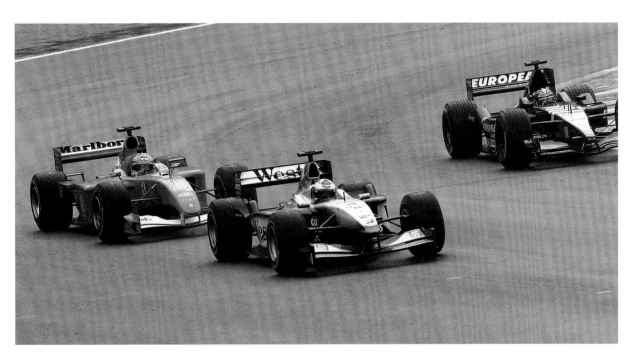

David appeared to be relishing the season, attacking Schumacher guns blazing in France and passing him with the universal gesture of contempt, the single, raised middle finger. The message was clear: David had had enough – enough of Schumacher's intimidatory driving tactics, enough of being Häkkinen's understudy, enough of being thought of as 'too nice'. It was as if McLaren's life force had ebbed from one side of the garage to the other, for as David flourished, Mika withered. In the first half of 2000 he seemed only a grey, grainy facsimile of his true self.

Ron Dennis could not countenance watching his protégé sully his immaculate image. He took Mika to one side and soon after excused him all McLaren duties – testing, PR, sponsor talks – post-France, until the next race, the Austrian Grand Prix. 'Winning two championships in a row takes a lot out of a driver,' said Dennis. 'I think that mentally Mika is exhausted and needs a break.'

It did the trick. And how. In Austria pole and win surrendered meekly to Mika. Just like the old days. Just like the old days, too, was what followed. A string of good results for Mika (second, first, first, second) coincided with a series of weaker finishes for David (third, third, fourth, retired) to move Häkkinen to the top of the championship table. With 80 points, he was two ahead of Michael Schumacher and 19 ahead of Coulthard. Yet again the championship initiative had slipped away from David and yet again the corporate might of McLaren-Mercedes was about to be exercised in Häkkinen's favour.

Jurgen Hubbert, the most senior executive involved in Mercedes's F1 operation, hinted David would be expected to support Häkkinen's drive for the championship in the last three grands prix: America, Japan and Malaysia. 'Due to David's accident in Monza [he had been taken out by a spinning Jordan] his chances are minimal. Therefore I would presume that we will concentrate from now on one driver.'

The decision was academic, as Michael Schumacher won all of the final three races, to take Ferrari's first drivers' title since Jody Scheckter had last achieved the feat in 1979. Häkkinen scored only nine points from those races, David 12, to finish second and third in the championship.

2000 had been David's most convincing season yet in F1, and his most successful in terms of wins, but still he was being made to feel like a number two, even when it was he who had carried the McLaren torch for much of the season. His frustration lay in the knowledge that even though he had raised his game and been able to capitalise on the occasional Häkkinen off-day, he had come up against a Schumacher-led Ferrari team which had finally discovered the knack of winning consistently and well. Ten red wins, nine of them for Schumacher, against seven for McLaren, split 4–3, told the story of the season. Ferrari's all or nothing support of Schumacher had trumped McLaren's even-handed ideal. Perhaps, after all, McLaren should have gathered behind David during Mika's mid-season slump.

He refused to allow such abstractions to detain him: 'Do I need to apologise that two guys on top of their form have been finishing in front of me? Can I not have the dream that I can improve to the point where I can beat them? Do I have to accept that I'm never going to, just because I haven't? I don't think I have.'[3]

This was fighting talk and the mood was catching. Norbert Haug, head of Mercedes's motorsport operation, had long been a supporter of DC and at the launch ceremony for McLaren's 2001 car, the MP4-16, he made his views clear: 'One day you guys will realise how good he is,' he told assembled journalists. 'I have seen David improve every time he has got in the car. People forget that it is tough to beat Michael Schumacher and Mika Häkkinen because both are

Victory in Brazil in 2001 showed David at his best: calm, composed, and ruthless. He seemed this year to be gathering the momentum required to mount a successful title bid.

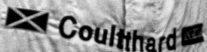

World Champions. But now Mika is saying it is tough to beat David.'[4]

There could be no doubting David's commitment to his – and McLaren's – cause. He chose to defer his marriage to Heidi Wichlinski in order that it did not distract him from racing. He worked on his fitness with renewed intensity and spent long hours during the off-season analysing telemetry from tracks, such as Suzuka, where he had always been slower than Häkkinen, and working out how he could close the gap. Ron Dennis appreciated the application: 'David's decision was based on thinking "How can I do better? How can I avoid being distracted?" It is just a desire to focus and I respect him for that decision.'[5]

There was an abundance of focus evident when David took his first win of the season, at the third round, the Brazilian Grand Prix. It is a race vivid in the memory for an outrageous third lap pass by F1 rookie Juan Pablo Montoya on Michael Schumacher, which brought the press room (and a global TV audience) to their feet.

Almost forgotten in the aftermath was an equally vivid pass by David on Michael at the start of the 50th lap. On a wet track, he squeezed through on an inside line into turn one, as the McLaren and Ferrari lapped the Minardi of backmarker Tarso Marques. The mood, the aggression, was reminiscent of that combative July day at Magny-Cours nine months earlier. David went on to pull away from Michael and win by 16 seconds. On a treacherous afternoon, David and Michael lapped every other runner.

Häkkinen's start to the year had been poor, with just one point so far for a sixth place in Malaysia. David, though, was flying. He had finished second, third, and first, in a McLaren that was still far from perfect, to position himself as Schumacher's most credible challenger. Behind the scenes at McLaren team members were acknowledging that Mika had lost some of his force, his rage to win. David was their best hope this season and they began to state it publicly. Post-Brazil, Ron Dennis described the win as 'David's finest race', while Norbert Haug positively gushed: 'Magny-Cours last year was a very similar race but the circumstances here were much more difficult as we did not know how heavy the rain was. This was David's victory because I am not sure we had the best car today – but he was the best driver and he handled the

With a little help from my friends . . . Mika hitches a lift after a last-lap engine failure in Spain.

Victory at the 2001 Austrian Grand Prix was further proof of David's race-winning abilities. He had taken on the mantle of *de facto* team leader with assurance, earning the renewed respect of all those in the team.

circumstances the best. David is not a number two, he is not even a "number one B". He is a clear number one just as much as Mika Häkkinen is.'

Genuine as his words were, Haug had revealed more than he realised about the McLaren team psyche. Why insist that David was 'not a number two' when no-one was asking the question?

Two weeks later, at the Spanish Grand Prix, the roles were reversed and some of the old tensions resurfaced. Häkkinen was immaculate all weekend. After qualifying second (to Schumacher) he tore into the far distance, and was set to win at a cruise when his clutch exploded within half a lap of the flag. David finished fifth after a problem on the warm-up lap which relegated him to the back of the grid. Ron Dennis later accused David of 'brain-fade', on live TV. When David heard of the remark the red mist descended. 'I think it is fair to say that Ron has had a bit of brain-fade to make that comment without talking to me or the engineers first,' he seethed. He quivered with tension as he spoke. A well of resentment was being given voice.

Alongside the soap-opera, a World Championship was being fought over, one in which Häkkinen's chances appeared to be fading fast. After five races, he had scored only four points. The calls for McLaren to ask Mika to back David were growing louder. They grew louder still after the Austrian Grand Prix, from notables including BMW motorsport director (and multiple grand prix winner) Gerhard Berger. David won the race with another lustrous display, holding off pressure from the Ferraris of Schumacher and Rubens Barrichello all race, and closing the gap to Michael, the championship leader, to just four points. Häkkinen failed yet again to score, after being left stranded on the grid with a failed launch control system.

It seemed inevitable that McLaren would move to back David. But no, said Dennis, 'both our drivers could still win the championship. Neither of them should even begin to believe they cannot win. They have a strong car with which they can win races and compete.' He spoke as a skilled team boss should: emollient; confident; even-handed. Over a quiet bowl of breakfast muesli in the grey-suede calm of his McLaren motorhome office, he confided, however, that

he had been deeply impressed with David's start to the year.

'He has made a quantum leap forward in his approach to Formula 1. He is doing a very good job and is more than able to do the task.' This, on the morning *before* David's win. As for the 'brain-fade' episode: 'Before saying "brain-fade" and immediately after saying "brain-fade", I had qualified that by saying I had not yet got all the data available. On a scale of one to ten, "brain-fade" as an expression used in the team would be a one or a two. It is a constantly used expression as an indication of a loss of concentration. Unfortunately, the media seized on it and made it appear a huge issue.'[6]

David was undeniably 'hot' in the first half of '01. The momentum gained from a strong opening half-dozen races was carried to Monaco, round seven. On the gilded boulevards of Monte Carlo, he annihilated the field in qualifying, to take pole position with a lap he will surely come to consider as his best ever. 'Anyone who can outqualify Mika Häkkinen and Michael Schumacher at Monaco has reason to feel very proud,' said Ron Dennis.

That Saturday night, the night before David's race turned to dust with another of the launch control glitches that had bedevilled McLaren's season, marked the zenith of David's career to date. He had beaten a double and a triple World Champion in a street-fight showdown and was breathing down Schumacher's neck in the race for the title. He had won here last year and had every reason to feel confident about his chances in the race. The future was unfolding before him. Everything seemed possible.

That he could only finish fifth after a ruined start that ensnared him for 35 laps behind the Arrows of Enrique Bernoldi was too cruel. Yet the weekend had been a perfect snapshot of the Coulthard career. Wonderful natural talent, resilience, courage, the ability to beat anyone on his day, but always being hauled back by the hand of fate just as the prize was within reach. After Monaco, his year fell apart. There were four retirements in the next ten races, and while there were another five podiums, including a second by stealth at Spa, there were no more wins. Over the same period

With pole position at Monaco in 2001 everything seemed possible. But David's race was ruined by electronic problems.

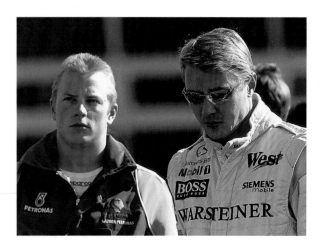

Schumacher and Ferrari became ever stronger, winning another five times, with two second places, to end the season as dominant champions.

Michael's haul was 123 points; David's 65, for second in the championship. It seemed hardly a fair reflection of David's magnificent early form, but there had been no answer to the red onslaught. McLaren and Mercedes accelerated development of their car and engine as hard as they dared, with the result that its reliability was further compromised. Norbert Haug would later admit the team 'had made mistakes' which scuppered David's title run.

Häkkinen, who finished a lowly fifth in the table, also won only twice. The second of those wins, at the penultimate race of the season, the US Grand Prix, turned out to be the last (Mika's 20th) of a majestic career. Since the start of the year McLaren sources had muttered that Häkkinen was thinking of retirement. His wife Erja had given birth to a baby son, Hugo, a year earlier and he admitted, to those who knew him well, that his desire to be with his family had started to outweigh his desire to race.

At the Italian Grand Prix the rumours were put to rest as he announced he would not race in 2002. It was not, he said, a retirement, rather, a 'sabbatical'. 'I simply want to enjoy a break,' he said. 'I think that if you look at the other drivers in history who have had a break they come back stronger. It's good just to take time off and recharge the batteries. You never know what might happen. I might like the break and would

like to have longer than a year. We will just have to wait and see.'[7]

He admitted soon after the end of the season that his family had become his priority. 'When I came back from Japan I took Hugo in my arms and realised that he is already almost one year old. How time flies. The months have gone and all that time since he was born have been spent talking about F1. When you are in a sport, that is so important and you must concentrate so much on it. But still, it is the family that is the most important thing in my life. I just want to enjoy having a chance to spend longer times with my wife Erja and my son without having to go somewhere else all the time.'[8] It was no surprise when he strolled into the paddock at Monaco six months or so later, toddler Hugo holding his hand, to announce that life as a full-time dad and husband suited him pretty well, thanks, and he would never race in F1 again.

The manner of his last win had been fitting. He took on and beat Michael Schumacher in a style so familiar from the '98 and '99 seasons, to leave F1 with an abiding memory that his speed had always been 100 per cent proof.

Mika's last win was also the occasion of the last race for McLaren's Jo Ramirez. The team had known for some time that he would be leaving and in recognition of his contribution over two decades, through Lauda, Prost, Rosberg, Berger, Senna, Mansell, Häkkinen, and DC, a farewell ceremony had been arranged at the Hungarian Grand Prix. His eyes sparkle at the memory:

'Ah, it was one of the most fantastic days in all my years there... David and Mika bought me a Harley-Davidson as a retirement present, which was fabulous. But it wasn't just the gift, it was the way they did it. It was my 60th birthday the weekend of the Hungary race and also my last year. They just wanted to make a gesture... but a Harley-Davidson! I had no idea what was happening. I didn't even know they knew it was my birthday.

'After qualifying, Ellen [Kolby, McLaren's head of communications] came over to the truck where I was and told me I was needed in the motorhome and that it was important. So I walked over and suddenly out of one door comes DC; out of the other comes Mika. I looked around and hundreds of photographers had appeared from nowhere. I thought, "OK, nice, where's the birthday cake they're about to plaster all over my face?"

'Then Mika produced a really expensive-looking leather jacket, which said "Harley-Davidson" over the back. I said to them – jokingly – "Ah, you shouldn't have, I've always wanted a Harley." But I had no idea! Then they hoisted me up onto their shoulders and suddenly I could hear this V-twin rumble – you know the noise that Harleys make – whup, whup, whup, whup. Then it was rolled up outside the motorhome, this huge, black Harley Road King. DC said to me, "Do you like it?" "Like it? I love it!" "It's yours!"

'Even now the memory of it gives me goosebumps. Maybe racing drivers don't have such long pockets after all. DC made all the arrangements and they paid for it together. I had never seen anything like that in all my years in the sport.'

There was a sense of shifting eras at McLaren in 2001. David had been signed for another two years (earning roughly £8 million a season), but Häkkinen's departure brought to an end the longest-lasting driver pairing in Formula 1. In his wake the team prepared to welcome his replacement, Kimi Räikkönen.

Another Finn, barely out of nursery school (he was 22, with only a single season of non-kart racing behind him), Räikkönen had made a great impression in his first F1 season with midfield team Sauber. Ron Dennis and his close advisers believed they saw in him the spark of a future World Champion and had signed him on a six-year deal. Häkkinen had seen the talent, too: 'I think he will push David right from the start.' A number of teams had shown interest in Räikkönen, but his management opted for McLaren, lured by the promise of 'joint number one' status.

Once again, and as always, David Coulthard would have to fight.

[1] www.bea-fr.org.

[2] *F1 Racing*, August 2000.

[3] *Autosport*, 2 November 2000.

[4] *Autosport*, 15 February 2001.

[5] Ibid.

[6] *Autosport*, 17 May 2001.

[7] *Autosport*, 20 September 2001.

[8] *Autosport*, 1 November 2001.

The 2003 Australian Grand Prix might have been one of David's luckiest wins, but who cares – at the end of the race, he was the guy on the top step, holding the biggest trophy..

tomorrow never knows

'I can see you Juan. You won't be coming through there. No way. Brake, brake, first gear, full lock, Loews hairpin – keep it tight – stroke throttle, gently, gently… power, power, power…'

Lap seven of the 2002 Monaco Grand Prix. David is leading the race. His car is fading, lapping slower at the front than is the Minardi of Alex Yoong in last place. Juan Pablo Montoya's Williams blankets the back of David's McLaren. Behind Juan is Michael Schumacher's Ferrari; behind *him* is the second Williams of Ralf Schumacher.

This cannot last. David's car looks like a tiring gazelle about to fall victim to a hunting panther. Barely surviving, it can taste the breath of its pursuer, feel its heat.

The Michelin tyres on David's car are 'graining' – losing grip before wearing into their best performance zone. The drop in performance is slowing David by two or three seconds per lap. Montoya is on Michelins too, but his car does not seem so badly afflicted.

He is desperate to pass David, having been on pole position after a vivid qualifying lap. David, who qualified second, had beaten Juan away from the line in a few seconds of sweet revenge for his startline failure a year earlier. He knows the routine at Monaco: stay ahead, make no mistakes and the win will come to you. Ayrton Senna showed Nigel Mansell how to do it back in 1992, holding off Mansell's far faster Williams for seven laps to take the win. But that had been in the desperate final stages of the race. Here, now, David has been under the kosh right from the start.

The pressure is immense, but the silver and black machine pacing around at the front exudes control.

… and after the race he was the guy getting the kiss from girlfriend Simone Abdelnour.

Monaco 2002: David threads his MP4-17 through the barriers to take his, and McLaren's, only win of the year. Montoya is right behind, pressuring David as his tyres lose performance.

David's team-mate Kimi Räikkönen looked certain to take his first F1 win at the 2002 French GP, but he half-spun on oil, allowing Michael Schumacher to take the win and the drivers' title.

David's thought processes are almost visible: as long as he keeps ticking off the sequence of steering, brake and throttle, he cannot be passed on this too narrow track. Or can he? There are 72 laps of this to go and the merest slip will bring calamity.

'Third, fourth, 125mph. Rascasse. Keep it tight, tight, right up to the barriers, carry the speed for the left-hander, stay in the middle of the track for the double-apex right. Blind. Bump on exit, keep stable…'

Monaco, more than any other Formula 1 track punishes mistakes. There can be no error. At least David's tyres have gone through their duff patch and are allowing him to lap once again at competitive speed – three seconds faster than before. He begins to edge away from Montoya and Schumacher.

Montoya's desperation to claim a race he believes he can win is obvious from his car's behaviour, as he clips barriers, locks wheels and slides the Williams sideways under power out of corners.

David remains calm, smooth, knowing that with Schumacher in third place, Juan Pablo is having to drive with an eye as much on defence as on attack. For the first time this season, a McLaren looks to be in control of a race. Monaco is the seventh grand prix of the year, and five of the first six have been won by Ferrari's Michael Schumacher. The only

non-Ferrari win has gone to Ralf Schumacher's Williams in Malaysia.

Few expect anything other than a Ferrari win at Monaco – Michael has won here five times already. As for his car … This year's Ferrari, the F2002, is emerging as more than merely dominant. Equipped with Bridgestone tyres designed to the specific requirements of Ferrari's chassis engineers and with handling tuned precisely to suit Michael's driving style, it is unstoppable. Yet David, remarkably, seems to be doing just that, halting the Schumacher-Ferrari bandwagon in its tracks despite the handicap of a less good car. It helps that David, too, is a Monaco ace, but he is obviously doing something a bit special to keep back two faster cars.

The laps tick by, slow as an egg timer for those aching to see the season enlivened by a non-Schumacher victory. Then, even as McLaren dare to dream, the curse of Coulthard looks as if it is about to intervene. On lap 30 smoke begins to puff from the exhausts of his MP4-17 under acceleration.

'I felt the engine start to tighten up,' said David later, 'and I was losing a bit of power. I radioed the team and they told me all the systems were working OK. I had to believe them.'

What happens next is worthy of *Thunderbirds*.

McLaren's engineers use electronic telemetry to communicate with the engine management system of David's car and succeed in remotely curing a problem with a transfer valve in the oil system.

When the fix is beamed in, David's lead is just over a second from Montoya. With a healthy car once more, he eases away again, to build a cushion of four seconds. That's the last he sees of Montoya, whose BMW engine blows on lap 46, allowing Schumacher through for a direct shot at DC. The attack never comes. For the only time this season, the Schumi-Ferrari F2002 combo is unequal to the challenge and David is clear to take his second Monaco win.

He never looked as if he would drop the ball and cheekily reveals later that he was so sure of victory, he laid out his ceremonial kilt on the bed before leaving his hotel room on Sunday morning – in preparation for the winner's gala dinner.

It was a great day for David, maybe his greatest, and the afterglow, while it lasted, was strong enough to burn away the spectre of Schumacher.

'Not many people get turned on by technology,' said Ron Dennis, 'but when you have it and you use it well it is a wonderful tool. It was tremendously satisfying to win like this.'

The Monaco result would be one of the few crumbs for David and his team in what was fast becoming a torrid year for all but Ferrari. When McLaren descended from their Monte Carlo cloud, they had to confront once again Michael's 40-point lead over David in the drivers' championship and Ferrari's 48-point margin over McLaren. Schumacher's Maranello cohorts went on to paint the season red in a manner not seen since Ayrton Senna and Alain Prost won 15 out of 16 races for McLaren in 1988.

The parade became a little tedious (not least for the 21 other drivers in Michael's wake!) and Schumacher duly won the title (his fifth) in record time, at the French Grand Prix in July. It was only round 11 of a 17-race season.

There was no shortage of irony in his title-winning victory coming at the expense of McLaren. The closing stages of the French Grand Prix had been controlled with dazzling efficiency by Kimi Räikkönen, David's new team-mate, who was in only his second season of Formula 1.

In this, his first year in senior school (after a kindergarten year at Sauber), Räikkönen had done everything expected of him: been sensationally fast; kept maximum pressure on DC and shown the spirit of a future champion Ron Dennis believed he had spotted a year earlier.

At Magny-Cours, in only his 28th Formula 1 race, he even took on head boy Michael in a manner most precocious, and looked to have had him beat, with five laps to go. An oil slick from the retired Toyota of Allan McNish, which caused Räikkönen to half-spin, scuppered his dream of a landmark maiden victory, but it mattered not: he had proven himself to be as fast as anyone out there and was certainly not shy of showing his far more experienced team-mate the way home.

This was tough for David. Not the fact of being beaten on the day (he finished third, Räikkönen second) – more the realisation that another year which had promised so much had faded into autumn, and earlier than ever before. Worse, he had not been able to establish himself as McLaren's undisputed number-one against a team-mate nine years his junior. Their qualifying tally at season's end was 10–7 in Kimi's favour and while David finished the year fifth in the drivers' championship, on 41 points, Kimi was right behind, on 24.

One well-placed McLaren source watched David's shoulders begin to sag when he realised Kimi was far more the finished article than he had any right to be, for one so young.

'With Mika gone, David felt that 2002 would be his big chance. But Kimi … we all knew he was quick, but we didn't realise just *how* quick he was going to be. He's one of those completely natural drivers. He doesn't know why he's quick but he just gets in the car and does it. He didn't have much idea about setting a car up, but that has always been one of DC's strengths, so he just followed David and then qualified even faster. That wasn't easy for David to watch. It was just the same for him with Mika.'

It wasn't meant to be like this. Post-Häkkinen, McLaren were meant to become *David*'s team. He had more than paid his dues. Now was the time for a little payback.

There had been hints from McLaren's ever-discreet management that they expected David to assume the mantle of *de facto* number-one, notwithstanding their policy of always according both drivers equal status: 'David has beaten Michael in the past and he can do it again,' offered Ron Dennis at the end of the previous season. 'We just have to provide him with the best equipment. He is more than capable of doing it.'[1]

Dennis's analysis said so much. Of course David was capable of beating Michael (he was the only man to do so in a straight fight all season); but of course he needed weapons for battle. The McLaren MP4-17 was not a good enough machine to take on the best Ferrari ever produced. It was blighted by a relatively weak Mercedes engine, forcing the team to spend much of the year 'trimming out' the chassis – running it with less downforce in a quest for competitive top speed. This made the car difficult to balance and delicate to drive. Only occasionally – as at Monaco and Magny-Cours – could it run at the front.

In pre-season testing MP4-17 had seemed fleet enough to renew David's hopes of a successful title shot. Once the teams reached Melbourne for the Australian Grand Prix, those hopes were crushed without ceremony, as the extent of McLaren's deficit became clear for the first time.

'That gave David a bit of a head problem,' said technical director Adrian Newey, 'but once he realised we didn't have a package to fight for the championship he just got on with enjoying the season on a race-by-race basis.'

Not that there was much to enjoy. After Monaco, there were only three more podium finishes: second at Montreal, then third at Magny-Cours and Indianapolis.

'It was difficult for me,' David admitted, 'the realisation that there was no championship potential, that we were lacking in … certain areas. Naturally, I try to avoid saying what they are, but we all know what they are! I had to change my focus. In the past, I'd never looked beyond the next race – but now I had to look at the bigger picture, to develop a car that was going to suit me better in the future.'[2]

So great was Ferrari's domination that Schumacher and team-mate Rubens Barrichello were far enough ahead, at the end of the American Grand Prix, to try to stage a dead-heat – to the disgust of US F1 fans and to the annoyance of the sport's governing body, the FIA. This act, and Ferrari's heavy-handed use of team orders earlier in the season at the Austrian Grand Prix, would have dramatic consequences later in the year.

Nürburgring 2002 was another difficult race in a difficult year for DC. As he attempted to pass Montoya, who was struggling with worn tyres, the pair clashed, putting both out of the race.

The win that got away. At Interlagos in 2003, David led the race and looked to be on his way to victory. But as he came into the pits the race was red-flagged after accidents to Mark Webber and Fernando Alonso (second and fourth in photograph). Had DC stopped a lap later, he would have won.

Their shenanigans were a world away from anything McLaren were ever in a position to achieve in 2002. Nonetheless Ron Dennis and the team around him – which included talents such as Newey, MD Martin Whitmarsh, and senior engineers Neil Oatley, Pat Fry, Mike Coughlan and John Sutton – were bullish about the future.

Plans for a radical MP4-18 were well advanced, as was a development programme for the existing car. Räikkönen had matured beyond expectation, while David would go into the off-season with confidence renewed from his strong finish to the year: the Indy podium was followed by a third-place qualifying spot at Japan's Suzuka circuit – the most challenging track of all.

David was entering his eighth season at McLaren, having turned down a potential big-money offer from F1 newcomers Toyota. Better, he said, to take the McLaren promise of performance over a fatter wage packet. Some close to him held their head in their hands at his stubborn refusal to chase the dollars, believing that the challenge from Räikkönen could only get stronger and that he should 'cash in his chips' while his F1 market value was still high.

But no: 'Why should I go to Toyota? Why go to an unknown quantity? There's no question this is absolutely the right place for me. Money is what you think about away from the race track. It should have no bearing on what you do at a grand prix.'[3]

Besides, David believed he was still getting better as a driver and that McLaren could only benefit from his presence. As well as accruing ever more experience, he was improving technically, he said, adding new skills to his repertoire, such as left-foot braking.

Throughout his career he had been a driver who braked with his right foot, as is customary on the road. But many racing drivers brake on the track with their left foot, teasing the car's stance as it slows, with tiny strokes of the throttle from the right foot, blending one against the other to extract maximum speed from the grip available. It is an intricate and unnatural technique – 'like writing with your left hand if you're right-handed' – and drivers who have not adopted it in their formative years tend to stick with what they know.

McLaren's much-heralded MP4-18 was a flop. It was due to be introduced early in the 2003 season, but serial failures meant it was never fit to race. Its absence blunted McLaren's championship campaign.

David, however, had seen how much time a left-foot braking Mika Häkkinen had been able to gain at corners such as the Suzuka esses and determined to follow suit. In practice for the 2002 Japanese Grand Prix, David relied on left foot braking for the first time, and it paid dividends in lap time and in mental strength stored for the winter.

If only he had known what lay ahead.

Storm clouds gathered around Formula 1 during the 2002–03 off-season. After a turgid year, dominated and at times manipulated by Ferrari, the sport's great and good were agreed that Something Had To Be Done to restore F1's appeal.

Smaller teams, such as Arrows and Prost, were going to the wall, unable to find budgets to compete with the leading runners. TV audiences were struggling to reach previous levels. A faint, but unmistakeable, scent of crisis crept into the rarefied air breathed by team principals and engine manufacturers.

The solution was dramatic. Limits were introduced on testing; the points system was altered to prevent a dominant team or driver from running away with the championship; the format of qualifying sessions was

changed to introduce single-lap 'shoot-outs' on Friday and Saturday.

Were David a paranoid individual, he might have looked at that last change and wondered what he had done to deserve it. More than most drivers, he had become used to using qualifying sessions to hone his car before going for the big time. Under the new format there would be no chance to do so, leaving the way clear for have-a go heroes like Räikkönen and Montoya. He would be forced every race weekend to play his weakest card.

So it proved at the Australian Grand Prix. David could only set 11th best time, with a lap he described as 'pretty average'. Deprived of the set-up time he was so adept at exploiting, he never felt comfortable. 'I can't attack with the car,' he said, 'I'm having to drive very defensively. When I tried to attack, I ran wide at the first corner. That set the tone for the whole lap.'

Räikkönen struggled too, qualifying only 14th, but come the race things were different. Rain fell half an hour before the start and David set off on wet tyres. Quickly though, the track began to dry and on lap two he came in to change to slicks and add fuel.

David rejoined in last place and looked to have a long, long afternoon ahead of him. Others on wets came in soon after David, then, on lap six, Jordan's Ralph Firman crashed heavily, bringing out the safety car.

As the field bunched up behind the Mercedes saloon with the flashing orange lights, David was already up to 11th place and his time deficit to the leaders had been wiped out. A second safety car followed on lap 17 and several of the lead bunch pitted for tyres and fuel. To general amazement, Räikkönen was now leading, with Schumacher second and David third. A further round of pit-stops followed, from which Montoya emerged in the lead, with Kimi second, Michael third and David fourth. Then the drama really began: a time penalty on lap 39 for Räikkönen; a splash 'n' dash fuel top-up for Schumacher on lap 46. With 12 laps to go David was second behind Montoya and would undoubtedly have settled for that on this crazy day. But it hadn't been that kind of race. When Montoya spun out of the lead on lap 48 – 'I just screwed up' – most had lost their capacity to be surprised at another twist in a madcap grand prix. And that, breathlessly, was that. David reeled off the last ten laps in a car that he had never been happy with, to

145

take the luckiest win of his career. As he graciously admitted: 'It wasn't one of my finer wins, but at the end I was standing in the middle of the podium between two talented drivers who'd had the same opportunities as me. I'll take it for what it is.'

It was a win to enjoy while it lasted, because at round two, the Malaysian Grand Prix, David was forced out with electrical failure. He had qualified an excellent fourth and made two places from the grid. The Renault ahead of him was running a pit-stop strategy which would have put it behind the McLaren over a race distance, so David, justifiably, felt robbed. Brilliant, but galling, was the win that followed for Kimi.

'When I ground to a halt I thought, "how many times has this happened when I'm in a podium position?" I would have run ahead of Kimi and you've got to presume that I'm not in the habit of making mistakes in the races.'

He wasn't – and he didn't, two weeks later, at a rain-lashed Brazilian Grand Prix. Even by the standards of what was becoming a wildly unpredictable season, this one had it all. Rubens Barrichello led his home race until running out of fuel. Michael Schumacher – peerless in wet conditions – lost control and crashed in a massive puddle. Fernando Alonso claimed third in an ambulance, after his huge lap 54 crash, which stopped the race. Kimi Räikkönen was awarded the win and Giancarlo Fisichella finished second. David had come into the pits from the lead a lap before the red flag was shown… A likely win had slipped away. It slipped away, too, for Räikkönen, after a protest from the Jordan team, and victory went instead to Fisichella.

Within McLaren a sense of déjà-vu was developing. Just as it had with Häkkinen, David could feel the team's axis beginning to shift slightly, in favour of his Finnish team-mate. With a little more good fortune he could have been in a commanding position at the head of the drivers' table: certain podiums, even wins, had gone begging and instead Räikkönen was taking the plaudits.

Not until the German Grand Prix in August, did David take another podium, but by then, all realistic hope of a title charge was over.

Compounding the disappointment was McLaren's failure to come to grips with their storied MP4-18. Great things had been expected of it, but testing had brought only serial mechanical failures. While the drivers felt it had promise, it was too raw to race, so the team continued all season with a developed version of the 2002 car: the MP4-17D. It competed remarkably well, and Räikkönen went to the final round with a chance of winning the title, only to be pipped by Schumacher.

Räikkönen's consistency and speed eclipsed David, who failed all year to adapt to the new qualifying format and whose car was less reliable than his team-mate's.

David's nadir came at the Nürburgring, for the European Grand Prix, where he could qualify only 9th in a car which Räikkönen found to be quick enough for pole position. The mood in the Coulthard motorhome, in which he stayed at all European races, was black that June night.

His continued struggle in qualifying (though not in races, where he was consistently a match for Räikkönen) had set paddock tongues wagging over his position within the team. David, hair shirt on, made no excuses: 'It just hasn't clicked for me. It is not a question of trying to re-do what I'm doing, but getting it right in qualifying. It is not like I'm being out-paced and out-raced, but at the moment I'm not getting enough from my results to make an impact. I'm going backwards relative to the championship leaders.'[4]

High above, the vultures were beginning to circle. Influential sources were hinting Montoya had been 'placed' at McLaren for 2004, leaving David out in the cold. The continued lack of a 2004 contract for DC was, they said, proof that McLaren were dissatisfied with his performance. Conspiracy theorists were further emboldened by smoke signals from Williams, where Montoya and his manager, Julian Jakobi, were said to be aggrieved at the relatively paltry $5m per season Montoya was paid in comparison to team-mate Ralf Schumacher's $13m. Jakobi, it was said, was attempting to threaten Williams with the departure of their star driver if they did not renegotiate his contract more favourably.

Williams have never taken kindly to being held to ransom by a driver, leading to further speculation that

McLaren and Williams might reach an accommodation over Montoya.

As the rumours spiralled, even Bernie Ecclestone, never normally one to pronounce publicly on the driver market, offered his thoughts: 'He's going to be like Tim Henman if he's not careful – good, but not quite there. Maybe if David did move it would be good for him.'[5]

Few were surprised when the announcement came from McLaren in mid-November that Juan Pablo would, indeed, be joining the team – but for 2005, not 2004. No statement was made as to who would partner him, although most observers believed Räikkönen the most likely candidate.

By now, David had agreed a year's extension to his McLaren contract, taking him through to the end of 2004. His future beyond that remained uncertain, but David refused to be fazed by the gossip-mongers: 'Every year there are rumours, it's not unique to this year. There is always pressure to get the job done and, whether you are at the beginning of your career on a one-year contract or whether you are on a multi-year contract in the middle of your career, it doesn't actually change a great deal. You have to perform and if there is a better option available then the chances are they will be in the car.'

Such resilience was quite remarkable under the circumstances; even more so was David's absolute refusal to acknowledge that the future was in any way clouded.

'I really think McLaren will take a big step forward in 2004,' he said. 'You might just have to write that British World Champion headline that you've been saving up for years and years.'[6]

Early one evening, in July 2003, David Coulthard's first manager, Tim Wright, gazes reflectively across the River Thames. Relaxing with a bottle of cold beer in the riverside garden of a south London pub, he lets the years roll away.

'You know,' he says, 'for a while in '95, when David started to make his mark, I really felt that we were in at the start of something special. David had everything: the image, the talent, the team. I had no doubt in my mind that he was the real thing. I was absolutely certain, in fact, he was going to be the next big thing – a new British sporting hero. David Coulthard was definitely going to be Britain's next World Champion…'

[1] *Autosport* 18.10.01

[2] *Autosport* 19/26.12. 02

[3] *Autosport* 18.07.03

[4] www.bbc.co.uk/sport

[5] www.bbc.co.uk/sport

[6] www.bbc.co.uk/sport

In the latter half of 2003, speculation mounted that Juan Pablo Montoya would be replacing David at McLaren in 2004 or 2005. In November it was announced that Montoya would join McLaren in 2005.

results

1983-5
Karting
Scottish Junior Kart Champion: 1983, 1984, 1985

1986-7
Karting
Scottish Open and British Super 1 Kart Champion

1988
Karting
Scottish Open Kart Champion

1989
Formula Ford
Winner of both Junior Formula Ford Championships
Third in Formula Ford Festival
Winner of the McLaren/*Autosport* Young Driver of the Year Award

1990
Formula Vauxhall Lotus/GM Lotus Euroseries
(Paul Stewart Racing)
Fourth, British Formula Vauxhall Lotus series
Fifth, GM Lotus Euroseries

Formula 1
Tests McLaren-Honda MP4/5

1991
British Formula 3 Championship
Second – five wins (Paul Stewart Racing)
Winner of the European Marlboro Masters of F3 at Zandvoort and the Macau Grand Prix

1992
F3000
Ninth in championship (Paul Stewart Racing) 11 points

Round	Venue	Grid	Race	Fastest lap
1	Silverstone	25	7	7th
2	Pau	7	DNF (accident)	-
3	Barcelona	12	8	-
4	Enna	11	DNF (electrics)	-
5	Hockenheim	9	DNF (accident)	-
6	Nürburgring	9	7	-
7	Belgium	8	4	-
8	Albacete	17	7	-
9	Nogaro	4	3	-
10	Magny-Cours	8	3	1st

Formula 1
Tests with Benetton-Ford

1993
F3000
Third in championship (Pacific Racing) 25 points

Round	Venue	Grid	Race	Fastest lap
1	Donington	13	13	-
2	Silverstone	9	2	1st
3	Pau	6	2	-
4	Enna	2	1	1st
5	Hockenheim	5	DNF (gearbox)	-
6	Nürburgring	6	7	-
7	Belgium	3	3	-
8	Magny-Cours	7	Spin	-
9	Nogaro	8	DNF (throttle)	-

Formula 1
Test driver for Williams-Renault

Le Mans
GT class winner for Jaguar

1994
F3000
Ninth in championship (one race for Vortex) 6 points

Round	Venue	Grid	Race	Fastest lap
1	Silverstone	3	2	-

Formula 1
Eighth in championship (Williams-Renault) 14 points

Round	Venue	Grid	Race	Fastest lap
5	Spain	9	DNF (electrics)	9th
6	Canada	5	5	9th
8	Great Britain	7	5	2nd

9	Germany	6	DNF (electrics)	1st
10	Hungary	3	DNF (spin)	3rd
11	Belgium	7	4	2nd
12	Italy	5	6	4th
13	Portugal	3	2	1st

Voted Scottish Sports Personality of the Year and ITV Young Sports Personality of the Year.

1995
Formula 1
Third in championship (Williams-Renault) 49 points

Round	Venue	Grid	Race	Fastest lap
1	Brazil	3	2	3rd
2	Argentina	1	DNF (electrics)	5th
3	San Marino	3	4	4th
4	Spain	4	DNF (gearbox)	3rd
5	Monaco	3	DNF (gearbox)	5th
6	Canada	3	DNF (spin)	22nd
7	France	3	3	4th
8	Great Britain	3	3	4th
9	Germany	3	2	2nd
10	Hungary	2	2	3rd
11	Belgium	5	DNF (gearbox)	1st
12	Italy	1	DNF (spin)	6th
13	Portugal	1	1	1st
14	Europe	1	3	2nd
15	Pacific	1	2	3rd
16	Japan	6	DNF (spin)	2nd
17	Australia	2	DNF (spin)	2nd

1996
Formula 1
Seventh in championship (McLaren-Mercedes) 18 points

Round	Venue	Grid	Race	Fastest lap
1	Australia	13	DNF (throttle)	16th
2	Brazil	14	DNF (spin)	16th
3	Argentina	9	7	11th
4	Europe	6	3	7th
5	San Marino	4	DNF (hydraulics)	4th
6	Monaco	5	2	5th
7	Spain	14	DNF (crash)	-
8	Canada	10	4	4th
9	France	7	6	7th
10	Great Britain	9	5	9th
11	Germany	7	5	4th
12	Hungary	9	DNF (engine)	11th
13	Belgium	4	DNF (spin)	6th
14	Italy	5	DNF (spin)	20th
15	Portugal	8	13	12th
16	Japan	8	8	7th

1997
Formula 1
Third in championship (McLaren-Mercedes) 36 points

Round	Venue	Grid	Race	Fastest lap
1	Australia	4	1	3rd
2	Brazil	12	10	10th
3	Argentina	10	DNF (crash)	-
4	San Marino	10	DNF (engine)	4th
5	Monaco	5	DNF (spin)	19th
6	Spain	3	6	3rd
7	Canada	5	7	1st
8	France	9	7	10th
9	Great Britain	6	4	11th
10	Germany	8	DNF (trans)	19th
11	Hungary	8	DNF (electrics)	12th
12	Belgium	10	DNF (spin)	17th
13	Italy	6	1	9th
14	Austria	10	2	3rd
15	Luxembourg	6	DNF (engine)	5th
16	Japan	11	10	5th
17	Europe	6	2	7th

1998
Formula 1
Third in championship (McLaren-Mercedes) 56 points

Round	Venue	Grid	Race	Fastest lap
1	Australia	2	2	2nd
2	Brazil	2	2	3rd
3	Argentina	1	6	4th
4	San Marino	1	1	2nd
5	Spain	2	2	3rd
6	Monaco	2	DNF (engine)	2nd
7	Canada	1	DNF (throttle)	2nd
8	France	3	6	1st
9	Great Britain	4	DNF (spin)	3rd
10	Austria	14	2	1st
11	Germany	2	2	1st
12	Hungary	2	2	5
13	Belgium	2	7	9th
14	Italy	4	DNF (engine)	3rd
15	Luxembourg	5	3	2nd
16	Japan	3	3	4th

1999
Formula 1
Fourth in championship (McLaren-Mercedes) 48 points

Round	Venue	Grid	Race	Fastest lap
1	Australia	2	DNF (hydraulics)	7th
2	Brazil	2	DNF (gearbox)	6th
3	San Marino	2	2	3rd
4	Monaco	3	DNF (gearbox)	7th

Round	Venue	Grid	Race	Fastest lap
5	Spain	3	2	4th
6	Canada	4	7	3rd
7	France	4	DNF (electrics)	1st
8	Great Britain	3	1	3rd
9	Austria	2	2	4th
10	Germany	3	5	1st
11	Hungary	3	2	1st
12	Belgium	2	1	2nd
13	Italy	3	5	4th
14	Europe	2	DNF (spin)	2nd
15	Malaysia	3	DNF (fuel pres)	14th
16	Japan	3	DNF (hydraulics)	3rd

2000
Formula 1
Third in championship (McLaren-Mercedes) 73 points

Round	Venue	Grid	Race	Fastest lap
1	Australia	2	DNF (engine)	14th
2	Brazil	2	D/Q	-
3	San Marino	3	3	3rd
4	Great Britain	4	1	4th
5	Spain	4	2	3rd
6	Europe	1	3	3rd
7	Monaco	3	1	2nd
8	Canada	2	7	4th
9	France	2	1	1st
10	Austria	2	2	1st
11	Germany	1	3	2nd
12	Hungary	2	3	4th
13	Belgium	5	4	2nd
14	Italy	5	DNF (crash)	-
15	USA	2	5	1st
16	Japan	3	3	3rd
17	Malaysia	3	2	4th

2001
Formula 1
Second in championship (McLaren-Mercedes) 65 points

Round	Venue	Grid	Race	Fastest lap
1	Australia	6	2	2nd
2	Malaysia	8	3	6th
3	Brazil	5	1	2nd
4	San Marino	1	2	2nd
5	Spain	3	5	4th
6	Austria	7	1	1st
7	Monaco	1	5	1st
8	Canada	3	DNF (engine)	10
9	Europe	5	3	6th
10	France	3	4	1st
11	Great Britain	3	DNF (susp)	18th

Round	Venue	Grid	Race	Fastest lap
12	Germany	5	DNF (engine)	8th
13	Hungary	2	3	2nd
14	Belgium	9	2	3rd
15	Italy	6	DNF (engine)	12
16	USA	7	3	4th
17	Japan	7	3	6th

2002
Formula 1
Fifth in championship (McLaren-Mercedes) 41 points

Round	Venue	Grid	Race	Fastest lap
1	Australia	4	DNF (gearbox)	4th
2	Malaysia	6	DNF (engine)	15th
3	Brazil	4	3	7th
4	San Marino	6	6	8th
5	Spain	7	3	3rd
6	Austria	8	6	8th
7	Monaco	2	1	4th
8	Canada	8	2	4th
9	Europe	5	DNF (crash)	9th
10	Great Britain	6	10	11th
11	France	6	3	1st
12	Germany	9	5	5th
13	Hungary	10	5	4th
14	Belgium	6	4	4th
15	Italy	7	7	3rd
16	USA	3	3	5th
17	Japan	3	DNF (throttle)	12th

2003
Formula 1
Seventh in championship (McLaren-Mercedes) 51 points

Round	Venue	Grid	Race	Fastest lap
1	Australia	11	1	5th
2	Malaysia	4	DNF (electrics)	7th
3	Brazil	2	4	4th
4	San Marino	12	5	5th
5	Spain	8	DNF (crash)	13th
6	Austria	14	5	5th
7	Monaco	6	7	7th
8	Canada	11	DNF (gearbox)	7th
9	Europe	9	15	6th
10	France	5	5	3rd
11	Great Britain	12	5	2nd
12	Germany	10	2	4th
13	Hungary	9	5	7th
14	Italy	8	DNF (fuel pres)	6th
15	USA	8	DNF (gearbox)	6th
16	Japan	7	3	2nd

index

Abdelnour, Simone 139
Adelaide 45, 54, 69, 75, 78, 103, 112
Alesi, Jean 20-21, 36, 39-40, 42, 50, 106
Alexandra Palace 99
Alliot, Philippe 46, 72
Alonso, Fernando 143, 146
Andretti, Mario 14, 41
Argentina GP
    1995 50, 53
    1998 114
Arnall, Mark 79
Arrows 99, 114, 134, 144
Ascari, Alberto 41
Australian GP
    1993 100
    1994 34, 45
    1995 52, 54, 70
    1996 72
    1997 100, 106, 108
    1998 109, 111, 113
    2002 142
    2003 138, 144
Austrian GP
    1997 106
    1999 120
    2000 130
    2001 132, 134
    2002 142
Autodromo Oscar Alfredo
    Galvez 50
Autosport magazine 44, 46, 62, 64, 77
    Awards dinner 103

Barcelona 11, 13, 15-16, 19, 127
Barrichello, Rubens 41, 46, 62, 81, 82, 84-85, 114-115, 118, 134, 146
Barrie, Jim 24
Bartels, Michael 90
Belgian GP
    1982 52
    1994 40-41
    1995 52
    1996 77
    1998 113-116, 118
    1999 121
Benetton 18, 20, 42, 45, 48, 50-51, 106, 114
Berger, Gerhard 36, 42, 44, 134, 136
Bernoldi, Enrique 134
Bishop, Matt 111, 114
Blundell, Mark 21, 50, 70, 72, 74
BMW 134
BMW.WilliamsF1 66
Boyce, Dave 28-30, 66
Brabham, Sir Jack 41, 100
Brack, Kenny 65

Bradshaw, Ann 12, 47
Brands Hatch 27, 57, 61-62
Brawn, Ross 114
Brazilian GP
    1994 12
    1998 114
    2001 128, 130, 132
    2003 143, 146
Briatore, Flavio 18
Bridgestone tyres 109, 117, 140
British GP
    1992 35
    1994 39-40
    1995 46
    1998 113
    1999 117
    2000 126, 129
Brundle, Martin 46, 72
Burt, Kelvin 61

Catalunya 11, 13, 127
Canadian GP
    1994 21, 33-35
    1995 50
    1997 100, 104
    1998 113, 116
    2002 142
Carman QC, George 47
Cawthorne, David 92
Clark, Jim 24, 41
Clear, Jock 40, 43
Cleveland, Ohio 39
Cockings, Dr Jerome 69
Contzen, Christian 33-34, 39
Cosworth engines 88-89
Coton, Didier 79
Coughlan, Mike 144
Courage, Piers 44
Coulthard, David
    crashes 65-66, 116-118, 120-121, 143
    diet 30
    driving skills 11, 20, 66, 84, 91, 142, 144
    education 29
    fastest laps 40, 53, 87, 115
    fitness 132
    F1 debut 15-16, 34, 48
    injuries 65-66
    interviews 75
    karting 20, 22-30, 50, 58, 61, 66
    plane crash 123-127
    pole positions 50-51, 53-54, 82, 115, 134
    PR duties 78
    qualifying problems 146
    race wins 32, 53, 62, 84, 87-88, 91-92, 95, 99-103, 106, 108, 114-115, 120, 122, 126, 128-129, 132, 134, 141, 146

test driving 10-12, 14, 16, 38, 62, 77, 85, 92
    McLaren Autosport Young Driver of the Year 46, 61-62, 64, 77
Coulthard, Duncan 20-21, 23, 26-29, 58
Coulthard, Duncan Jnr 23-24, 26
Coulthard, Joyce 20-21, 23, 26
Coulthard, Lynsay 23-24, 26, 28, 31, 127
Cunningham, Iain 66

David Coulthard Museum 13, 23, 31, 61
de Ferran, Gil 29, 38, 64-66, 78, 82, 85, 91
Dennis, Lisa 69
Dennis, Ron 18, 20, 43-46, 50, 54, 61, 63, 69-70, 72, 74, 79, 94, 101, 103, 106-107, 109-112, 117, 121, 127, 130, 132, 134, 137-146
Domenicali, Stefano 115
Donington 61, 82, 91
Donnelly, Martin 88
Dunlop Star of Tomorrow
    series 61

Ecclestone, Bernie 14, 33-35, 52, 103, 147
Enna 86-87, 91-92
Estoril 12, 53-54, 77-78, 99
European GP 115
    1994 34, 42, 44
    1995 53-54
    1999 117, 121
    2003 146
Fangio, Juan Manuel 41
Farina, Giuseppe 41
Farmer, Tom 81
Ferrari 20, 36, 39-40, 42, 44, 50, 52, 92, 97, 99-100, 116, 130, 132, 139-146
FIA 16, 18, 142
Firman, Ralph 92, 145
Fisichella, Giancarlo 95, 146
Fittipaldi, Emerson 41, 81
Formula Ford 26-27, 31, 56-62
Formula Ford Festival 59, 62
Formula Opel Lotus Euroseries 65
Formula Vauxhall Lotus 38, 63, 65-66, 81-82, 85
Formula 3 30-31, 38, 41, 62-63, 81-87, 91
Formula 3000 11, 13, 21, 29, 38, 48, 63, 85, 87, 91-92
Foubister, Peter 62-63
French GP
    1994 34, 38-39
    1995 50

2000 129-130
2002 140-141
2003 115
Frentzen, Heinz-Harald 39, 99-101, 106, 112, 117-118
Fry, Pat 144
F1 Racing magazine 75, 111, 114

Gallagher, Mark 90, 92
Gene, Jordi 82, 87
German GP
    1994 40
    1995 51
    2003 146
Goodman, Peter 33
Gribbin, George 27
Grovewood Award 63
Guerrier, Anna 112

Haas, Carl 14
Häkkinen, Erja 79, 136
Häkkinen, Hugo 136
Häkkinen, Mika 16, 20-21, 40, 43, 46, 54, 72, 74, 77 -79, 85, 96-97, 99, 102-121, 126, 132, 134
    Adelaide accident 69-70, 72, 77-78, 112
    Driver's titles 115, 118, 129
    pole positions 109, 130
    race wins 95, 107, 109-110, 115, 130, 136
    retirement 136
Harrison, George 103
Haug, Norbert 70, 100, 102-103, 130, 132, 134, 136
Haymarket Publishing 62
Hayton Coulthard Ltd 24, 81
Head, Patrick 13, 18, 33, 35, 42, 48, 92
Herbert, Johnny 100, 114
Higgins, Derek 29
Highland Spring 81
Hill, Damon 11-14, 16, 19-21, 33-36, 38-45, 47-48, 50, 53, 75, 95, 99, 105, 113-114
Hill, Georgie 13
Hill, Graham 13, 44
Hill, Phil 41
Hines, Martin 30
Hockenheim 91
Hogan, John 96
Hubbert, Jurgen 130
Hungarian GP
    1994 40
    1995 52
    2001 136-137

IMG 45-46, 75, 90
Imola 12-13, 16, 18-19, 50, 78, 114, 120

Indianapolis 500 race 14, 52
Indianapolis 142
Indycars 14, 34, 39, 52, 72
Irvine, Eddie 100, 113-114, 117-121
Italian GP
    1994 40, 42
    1995 51, 53
    1997 101, 105
    1998 112, 116, 118
    2001 136

Jaguar Racing 96
Jaguar XJ220 80, 91
Jakobi, Julian 146
Jamiroquai 99
Japanese GP
    1994 34
    1995 54
    1997 106
    1998 116-118
    2000 130
    2002 144
Jerez 16, 34, 44-45, 77, 88, 105, 107, 110, 113
Jordan 41, 78, 116-117, 117, 130, 145
Judd engines 87, 88-89

Kirkudbright Academy 29
Knockhill 57-58, 61
Kolby, Ellen 137
Kwik-Fit 81

Lakin, Scott 66
Lambert, Brian 11
Lamy, Pedro 11, 91-92
Larkhall 26-27, 30
Lauda, Niki 41, 136
Le Mans 80, 91
Lehto, JJ 20-21
Leslie, David 27, 57-58, 61, 63
Leslie, David Jnr 27, 57-58, 61, 63
Luxembourg GP 1997 106

Macau GP 1991 85-87
Magnussen, Jan 72, 77
Magny-Cours 38, 89, 126, 132, 142
Malaysian GP
    2000 130
    2001 132
    2002 140
    2003 146
Mansell, Nigel 14, 16, 21, 33-36, 38-39, 41, 44-45, 47-48, 50, 72, 74, 81, 136, 139
Marlboro 96
Marlboro Masters of Formula 3 85
Marques, Tarso 132
Matthew, Andy 123, 126
Mayell, Duncan 33
McLaren 11, 18, 20, 40, 43, 45-48, 50, 54, 62, 64, 69-70, 74-75, 77-78, 94-97, 99-104, 106-107, 112, 114-116, 125, 128, 130, 132, 134-147
    MP4/10 50, 72, 74, 77
    MP4/11 77
    MP4-12 95-96, 99, 106

MP4-13 109, 112
MP4-15 129
MP4-16 130
MP4-17 140, 142
MP4-17D 146
MP4-18 144-146
McLaren-Mercedes 96-102, 106, 130, 136
McNish, Allan 20, 27-30, 42, 58, 66, 142
McRae, Alistair 27
McRae Colin 27
Mehry Neto, Eduar 82
Melbourne 75, 94, 99-100, 103-104, 106, 109
Mercedes-Benz 45, 70, 77, 96-97, 100, 102, 105, 130
    engines 72, 96, 99, 101, 106, 109
Michelin tyres 139
Miller, Andy 82
Minardi 114, 132, 139
Monaco GP
    1969 44
    1994 13, 19, 33, 69
    1995 50, 72
    1996 78
    1997 104
    1998 113, 116
    2000 122, 129
    2001 82, 134, 136
    2002 139-142
    2003 48
Montermini, Andrea 19
Montoya, Juan Pablo 128, 132, 139-147
Montreal 35, 104
Monza 42-43, 53, 101, 105-106, 115, 118, 121, 130
Mosley, Max 18
Moss, Stirling 84
Motoring News 87
MTV 19
Murray, Andrea 14, 21, 91
Murray, David 123

Nakano, Shinji 114
Newey, Adrian 48, 54, 77, 97, 104-106, 109, 120, 142, 144
Newman-Haas 14, 34
Noda, Hideki 82, 85
Nogaro 89
Nürburgring 54, 91, 106, 117, 142
Nuvolari, Tazio 52

Oatley, Neil 144
Oulton Park 53

P&O Ferries Championship 61
Pacific GP 1995 53
Pacific Racing 31, 88, 90, 92
Paddock Club 13, 20
Palhares, Nico 62
Panis, Olivier 11, 92, 100, 104-105, 118
Patrese, Riccardo 15
Pau 91
Paul Ricard 12, 78, 109
Paul Stewart Racing (PSR) 29, 53, 63-64, 66, 81-82, 86-92

Philip Morris 96-97
Pickworths lawyers 33
Piquet, Nelson 81
Plasch, Alain 65
Portuguese GP
    1994 40, 42, 44
    1995 32, 53
Prost GP 104, 114, 118, 144
Prost, Alain 11, 33, 39, 41, 77-78, 112, 136, 141

Räikkönen, Kimi 136-137, 140-147
Ralt RT35 81
Ramirez, Jo 45-46, 72, 74, 99, 103, 109, 115
Ratzenberger, Roland 13, 16, 19
Renault 13, 16, 34, 39
    engines 21, 33, 48, 72
Renault Sport 33
Reynard 92D 89
Reynard-Cosworth 31
Ribeiro, Andre 82
Rosberg, Keke 136
Rothmans 12-13, 33
Rowrah track 26
Rydell, Rickard 82, 87

San Marino GP
    1994 13, 16, 19
    1995 50
    1996 74
    1998 111, 114
Sauber 69, 100, 114, 137, 141
Saunders, David 123
Scheckter, Jody 41, 81, 130
Schumacher, Michael 12, 15-16, 20, 36, 38-39, 41-42, 44-45, 48, 50-51, 53-54, 78, 85, 95, 99-101, 104-105, 107, 113-117, 119-120, 123, 126, 128-129, 132, 134, 136, 139-146
Schumacher, Ralf 114, 118, 140, 146
Scottish Junior Karting Championship 22, 26
Senna, Ayrton 11-13, 15-16, 33, 35, 38-39, 41, 48, 50, 70, 77, 81, 85, 99, 103, 112, 136, 139, 141
Silver Arrows 97
Silverstone 13, 37, 39, 42, 50, 52, 61, 65, 84-85, 89, 91, 105, 115, 120, 128-129
Simtek 19
Smith, Brian 12
Spa-Francorchamps 29, 37, 41, 65, 72, 78, 89, 90-92, 115, 118, 121, 134
Spanish GP
    1994 13, 15, 18-19, 33, 35, 50
    1995 72
    2000 125, 127, 129
    2001 134
Spice Girls 99
Stallone, Sylvester 18
Stewart, Sir Jackie 24, 29, 41, 52-53, 63-66, 81-82, 84, 129
Stewart, Paul 29, 63, 65-66, 81-82, 84, 86, 91

Stewart Grand Prix 63, 114
Stranraer 26-27, 30
Stubbs, Dave 86, 88
Surtees, John 41
Sutton, John 144
Suzuka 119, 132

Thruxton 61, 84-85
Todt, Jean 115
TOMS Toyota 82
Toyota 142, 144
Tremayne, David 118
Trulli, Jarno 129
Tunnock's biscuits 81
TWR 91
Twynholm 13, 23-24, 31
Tyrrell 21, 114

US GP
    2000 130
    2002 142

Van Diemen 26, 61
    RF89 31, 58
Villeneuve, Gilles 52
Villeneuve, Jacques 52-53, 74, 95, 99-100, 105, 107, 112, 114
Vortex 13

Walkinshaw, Tom 80
Watkins, Prof Sid 69
Webber, Mark 143
Wendlinger, Karl 19, 69
West 96-97, 105
West of Scotland Kart Club 27
West, Richard 33-35
West Surrey Racing 82
Whitmarsh, Martin 72, 144
Wichlinski, Heidi 123, 126, 132
Wiggins, Keith 88, 90-91
Williams, Sir Frank 12-15, 18, 21, 33-34, 39, 43-44, 48, 53, 70, 85, 104
Williams 10-13, 33-35, 38-40, 42-43, 45-47, 50-52, 54, 69-70, 72, 75, 77-78, 92, 94, 97, 99-101, 103, 106-107, 114, 120, 139, 146-147
    Constructor's title 11, 48
Williams-Renault 13, 16, 33, 44, 48, 100
    FW15 12, 16, 19
    FW15C 11
    FW16 16, 18, 21, 38-39
    FW17 48, 69
    FW19 99
Williams, Stewart 87
Windsor, Peter 111
Worley, Dan 123
Wright karts 30
Wright, Jim 66
Wright, Tim 45-47, 74, 90, 92, 147
Wurz, Alex 114

Yoong, Alex 139

Zandvoort 85
Zip karts 30
Zolder 64